Raised IN THE MILITARY

RAISED BY A MOM
SERVING IN THE ARMED FORCES

PATRICIA QAIYYIM

First paperback edition 2026

Book cover: Neakail Tolbert
Editing: S. G. George

ISBN (paperback): 979-8-9871951-5-4
ISBN (E-book):   979-8-9871951-6-1

Published by Patricia Qaiyyim
www.patriciaqaiyyim.com

Library of Congress Control Number: 2025922477

The views expressed in this literary work are those of the author and children raised by members of the Armed Forces, and do not necessarily reflect the official policy or position of the United States (U.S.) Government or Armed Forces.

DEDICATION

To my children, who started their lives as "military brats," who endured life in the military while their parents pursued their careers, and for their support and 'service' as members of a military family.

To my husband and partner, whose love and support continue to empower me to pursue my dreams.

To all the children who were raised in the military, are being raised in the military, and will be raised in the military. Thank you for your support and for doing your part as a member of a military family.

TABLE OF CONTENTS

Life in the Military 9

ACRONYMS/DEFINITIONS 10

PREFACE.. 12

FOREWORD... 14

Chapter 1: Motherhood in the Military.............................. 17

Chapter 2: The Military Brat 23

Chapter 3: A Child's Perspective on Their Mother's Service 29

Chapter 4: Living The Military Lifestyle............................ 39

Chapter 5: We're Moving Again... 49

Chapter 6: While You Were Gone 61

Chapter 7: The Best Parts 73

Chapter 8: The Worse Parts.. 83

Chapter 9: Following The Military Path? 91

Chapter 10: One Piece of Advice.. 101

ACKNOWLEDGEMENTS... 113

REFERENCES.. 114

ABOUT THE AUTHOR... 117

LIFE IN THE MILITARY
YOUR PARENTS' CHOICE

I chose, for a while, to serve my country by wearing the uniform.
For you, as my child, life in the military was simply your norm.

No one asked you if life in the military was right for you.
And like me, in your own way, you served too.

There were sacrifices that we all had to make.
Me, for the nation; and you, for my sake.

You grew up living a life that, for many, may have seemed unusual or strange.
This life you lived, for my service, was the greatest exchange.

My service had you moving so often and leaving friends yet again.
Getting to spend time with family only now and then.

Believe it or not, of your sacrifices, I was always aware.
And every decision I had to make, I did it with care.

You didn't get to choose me as your parent, or the career that I chose.
And I know that life in the military came with its highs and its lows.

In the end, when you are on your own,
and look back on the life that I gave you.
I hope your experiences were good,
your memories happy, and your regrets but a few.

Patricia Qaiyyim

ACRONYMS/DEFINITIONS

Active Duty: Full time service in the armed forces

Armed Forces: Six distinct branches—Army, Marine Corps, Navy, Air Force, Space Force, and Coast Guard—under the Department of Defense

Basic Training: The initial training received by enlisted members upon entry into the Armed Services

Command (Chain of Command): Hierarchical chain of leadership that one follows

Commissioned: Duty as a commissioned officer in the pay grade of O-1 through O-10

Deployment (Deploy): The movement of military personnel to various locations for possible military action

Deployment Return Date: Date deployers are scheduled to return from deployment; this date can fluctuate days or weeks

Enlisted: Duty as an enlisted member of the Armed Forces, in the pay grade of E-1 through E-9

First Sergeant: First Sergeant is a duty position held by Air Force members in the rank of E-7 through E-9, works with, advises, and reports directly to the unit commander on matters of enlisted morale, welfare, and conduct.

Junior Reserve Officers' Training Corps (JROTC): Military-supported, high school-based education program focusing on leadership, citizenship, and personal responsibility

Military Brat: Child whose parent(s) are in the Armed Forces

Military Installation (Base) (Post): Locations (installations) around the world where members of the Armed Forces are stationed

Orders: Military instructions; can be written or oral. Military orders are used to assign members to military installations.

PCS: Permanent Change of Station, moving from one permanent location to another

Personnelist: Manages, advises on, and processes military personnel programs, policies, and records

Remote (Unaccompanied) Assignment: An assignment to a location without family members, not a deployment, usually twelve months or longer

Reserve Officers' Training Corps (ROTC): A college-level program training students to become commissioned officers in the U.S. Army, Navy, Air Force, or Marine Corps while earning a degree

TDY: Temporary Duty: Temporary period of time away from your permanent duty location, usually for training, conferences, medical treatment, etc.

PREFACE

A few decades ago, the Armed Forces gave little thought or consideration to the children of service members. Their needs were considered secondary, family was the parents' responsibility, and military obligations came first. American author Pat Conroy grew up the son of a Marine Corps officer. He moved eleven times before he was fifteen. When discussing his experience, he once wrote, "We spent our entire childhoods in the service of our country, and no one even knew we were there."[1]

In the 1980s, the Department of Defense and our Armed Forces officially recognized the role and sacrifices of military children, affectionately known by some as military brats. Over the years, the term "military brat" has evolved from a casual label to a badge of honor, recognized by many military parents, teachers, and members of military communities, regardless of which branch of the Armed Forces one serves. For many of these children, being a military brat has become a shared identity, a way to recognize each other in a world where most civilians cannot fully understand their lifestyle.

Military brats are considered part of the military family and as an extension of their parents' service. Today, they are formally celebrated. April is the Month of the Military Child, and according to the Department of Defense, as of 2025, there were 1.6 million military children.[2] Their lives are often quite different from the lives of many other children in the United States.

Military brats grow up on or near military installations. They often grow up hearing the Star-Spangled Banner (national anthem) regularly, participate as spectators in military events, attend schools run by the Department of Defense, and will move several times during their young lives. They have the opportunity to experience life in foreign countries and have to endure separation from their military parents due to Temporary Duties (TDYs), deployments, and remote assignments.

In my first book, *Moms in the Military: Raising a Child while Serving in the Armed Forces*, I interviewed twenty military moms about parenting while serving in uniform. At some point they all wondered what kind of impact their career choice might have on their children.

Most of us, when looking back on our childhoods, have memories of weekend get-togethers with family, regular dinners with grandparents, visiting aunts and uncles, and hanging out or sleepovers with cousins. But for military brats, their memories might include moving every few years, being the new kid over and over again, visiting family only once or twice a year, and even feeling more like strangers than family when they do.

This made me wonder: do military children look back on this life with pride or regret? With fondness and good memories or with anger and frustration? How do they honestly feel about their childhood, and would they feel proud of their identity as a military brat? Would they think that it was too many sacrifices? I couldn't answer these questions, but the military brats who lived it could.

I interviewed eighteen adults and children raised by one or both parents who served or are serving in the Armed Forces. This book is a compilation of their stories, their insights, and their experiences growing up in a military family. My hope is that their words will shed light on a lifestyle few civilians understand, give voice to military children everywhere, and offer encouragement to children navigating similar journeys today.

FOREWORD
By Robyn Tresnak, PhD

Growing up in a military home and now the parent of a service member, Raised in the Military invoked emotions and insight that led me to reflect in fantastic ways. Written with Patricia's thoughts, coupled with the quotes of children raised in military families, my mind soared across personal decades. How wonderful it is to see her questions and the personal answers from children of all ages who have been through such varied experiences in the military.

As the words traveled from my eyes to my brain, to my heart, I pictured thousands of experiences throughout my childhood. I sensed immense feelings from childhood to today. One comment in these pages shared the norm of the child who was "afforded numerous opportunities," which precisely describes my life as a child of an army officer. Patricia supported this thought in her poem, noting that it was the norm for children basically to serve alongside their parents. She wondered if her own children, and so many others, thought of their military childhood as a gift or burden. Personally, I found great pride; I saw it as a delightful gift. Without going into details of personal stories, I can say with confidence that I have pictures of each assignment across the states and abroad that added to who I am today.

Patricia's writing and book design also sent me to thoughts of my son, both the way he grew up, his beginning years in the army, and the future he plans to continue in the service. From travels to army posts, to visits to army hospitals, to stories of military pasts, my son has been a part of it all. Through it all, he chose a career in the army. This was his path fairly early. He planned college around the army. He planned grad school around the army. He and his now wife planned a future around the army. I can say with confidence that I have pictures of each of his steps that added to who I am today and who he is today.

There are many times now when I sit back and watch the connections between my dad's full, twenty-three-year career as an army officer and my son's opening five years as an army officer. My son is making his own path in the army yet following similar footsteps. It was a treasure to watch my dad share the commissioning moment with my son; a photo that will stay in my mind forever, as well as both of theirs. That moment provokes tears of joy, along with influences of strength, patience, integrity, and determination. Earlier this year, five years from that commissioning, I visibly noticed another connection. I stood at a distance and watched as my dad and son stood at attention, with the exact same stance, during the changing of the guard at the Tomb of the Unknown Soldier. This was one of many connections from the last five years, and I trust one of many more on our journey.

Yes, I mentioned "our journey" previously. No matter the stage of life, a military family finds a way to journey together. As I read Patricia's words in *Raised in the Military*, I recognized the journey she took as a service woman, military spouse, and mother of military children. I recognized the journey she still takes today with her children even in military retirement, the way she considers their next steps, and the way she strives to impact the lives of so many other military children, military families for the strength of their futures.

As you read this amazing account of living through various stages in the military family, consider the journey. As Patricia shares, the journey is paired with challenges and joys that give growth and pride. Think about those who serve our country through a portion of their journey. Think about how your journey is impacted by the military family. Think about ways you touch the lives of military families. Think about a route in your journey that could share time with military families to glean and grow together. Patricia offers a beautiful account of the journey through both the mind of the military child and parent. Thank you, Patricia, for presenting your words, along with those who were raised in the military and contributed to this book.

Chapter 1:
MOTHERHOOD IN THE MILITARY

"The greatest gifts you can give your children are the roots of responsibility and the wings of independence."[3]

—Denis Waitley

When I joined the Air Force, I didn't think about children. In fact, I didn't even consider marriage. I was at the beginning of my career in the Air Force and focused on learning how to succeed in a world built on structure, discipline, and sacrifice. However, within two years I found myself standing at a crossroads, motherhood while serving in uniform or separating and transitioning back to civilian life. I had a few months to decide if I could, or even wanted, to tackle raising a child and active duty simultaneously. I knew I wanted to continue serving my country, and I couldn't imagine what I would have done if I had become a civilian again.

For me, this decision was the first serious choice I had to make that would have impact on another human being, and I chose both. I chose both because I truly wanted to serve my country in the Air Force and I wasn't ready to give up fulfilling my dream and career. I didn't want to regret not pursuing my dream of serving in the Armed Forces. I served more than twenty years in the Air Force. During many of these years, like many other women in uniform, I navigated the complex balance of motherhood and military service.

I often remember when my children were small, they enjoyed putting on my uniform shirt or hat. Most certainly, it was a way of imitating what they saw. When I watched them playing with or trying to put on my military gear, which was too big for their little bodies, I knew they didn't understand that I was willing to die in those clothes to ensure that they had life free from tyranny. They had no way to know that during military exercises, we spent days training, not just how to do our jobs, but how to defend the installation, how to protect ourselves and our fellow Airmen, all to prepare ourselves to survive in combat situations on foreign soil. To them, it was simply something different, and when I brought my gear out of the closet, it was just an indicator of longer days for Mom and Dad. I found that as they grew older and gained a better understanding of the gasmask, helmet, flak vest, and chem gear, they no longer viewed my military gear as something exciting or fun.

Their childhood, like that of many military brats, entailed moving every few years, not just from one house to another, but from one state to another, and sometimes to another country altogether. This always meant leaving friends and familiarity behind. Sometimes, they were ready to move and excited about the next adventure, and other times, they were steadfast in their desire to stay.

Our family's packing up and moving was not the only challenge they had to deal with. Sometimes, it was their friends, who were also part of military families, packing up and taking off for their own "'next adventure."

But one of the hardest parts, at least for me, was when my husband, a retired veteran and Department of Defense civil servant, was stationed at a different installation than us over the Christmas holiday when my children were eight, nine, and seventeen. I count myself lucky that we were able to video call my husband and open presents together, even if we were half a world apart. Our family was fortunate that at least one of us was almost always around to watch our kids. Others were not as fortunate, and it is not uncommon for children whose parent(s) are away on deployment to end up living with aunts, grandparents, or even under the care of other members of their military community.

Military moms, like moms everywhere, make the best decisions they can for their children with regards to the things over which they have control. Are these choices, in fact, the best ones? Not always, but they are always made with the best intentions—for our families, for our careers, and for the life we've chosen to build.

I sometimes questioned if the military lifestyle was a good life for my children. They may not have signed up for military life, but they lived it just the same. Would my decision to serve ultimately help them or hurt them?

Like me, many other military moms I spoke with also carried the weight of that question. We asked ourselves if the Armed Forces was the right environment to raise a child. For many of us, the answer was, without a doubt, a resounding yes.

There were times when I actually questioned if the sacrifices were too much for them. But, in the end, I could see that they adjusted to this life of frequent moves, goodbyes, and separation; that the love and home that we created gave them the tools to deal with life as military brats.

As they got older, I could see that my military service even had a positive impact. It has helped them develop a sense of pride in being a citizen of the United States, a sense of resilience that enabled them to cope with many of life's challenges, and a sense of adventure that encouraged them to be open to change and new opportunities.

My son travel to Sapporo Japan for the Sapporo Snow Festival when he was eleven years old, brave and curious, ready to experience a host family in a foreign land. My youngest did not think twice about going away to camp just months after relocating. And I saw the excitement and courage when my oldest daughter headed off to college halfway across the nation without hesitation. In fact, in all situations, my children showed how comfortable they were with change, confident in their ability to adapt. I am sure that I felt more hesitant and worried than they did.

In researching and interviewing other military moms, they shared similar stories with me, both good and bad, about their children's lives as military brats, from separation during significant events to missing extended family members to their parents' deployment-return date being pushed out. There were stories of pain, like one mom's story about her young child developing separation anxiety after a remote assignment that lasted over a year. But also, stories of their resilience, like one mom whose young child was almost inconsolable during one deployment and later, in his early teens, saying goodbye before a deployment with, "Mom, you got this."

As I look back on my career and my children's lives growing up, I am confident that my choice to tackle military service and motherhood simultaneously was the right choice. My career in the Air Force came with lots of experiences, in and out of the U.S. I met wonderful people along the way, those who mentored me and those I was lucky enough to mentor. I met people from all over the world, and I enjoy relationships that have weathered separation and time.

But this book isn't about me, it is about my children and other children who are or have grown up with a mom serving in the Armed Forces. Similarly, each child has encountered unique experiences and formed friendships influenced by their upbringing within a military environment and what comes with life in the military. This is their story and I am honored to help them tell their stories.

Chapter 2:
THE MILITARY BRAT

"Like dandelions, military children bloom everywhere the wind carries them. They're ready to fly in the breezes that take them to new adventures, new lands, and to meet new friends."

—Author Unknown

On a military installation, everyone has an identifier. Words like active duty, reservist, enlisted, commissioned, military spouse/dependent, civil servant, and government contractor are commonly used. Just as these words give identity to the adults working and living on the installation, *military brat* gives identity to military children. It also identifies their role within the military family and community.

The term *military brat* has a long history and has long been accepted as a term of endearment to describe children of military parents. Some believe this term has been around for centuries, and there are several theories about its origin.

A book published in 1921 attributed the saying to the British army. It explained *B.R.A.T.* as a status standing for *British Regiment Attached Traveler*, assigned to families who could travel abroad with a soldier. Eventually, it just referred to military children. The term stuck and was adopted in many places around the world, including the United States. Another publication traces *Army brat* back to 1942, when it appeared in a military slang publication called *The War Dictionary*. It defined the term specifically regarding the children of Army officers and stated that it was a term of endearment.[4]

Regardless of when the term military brat started or by whom, today, military brat is synonymous with military children throughout the Armed Forces. They are formally celebrated on installations and in communities around the globe. They are recognized locally for their outstanding contributions and awarded scholarships, and at the national level, some receive the Military Child of the Year Award.

Communities on and off military installations are celebrating military children. One way is through Purple Up campaigns. Purple represents all service branches. It blends each branch's colors: the Air Force, Navy, Space Force, and Coast Guard's blues, the Army's green, and the Marine's red. Wearing purple symbolizes unity among military children across all services and reminds them that they are supported and seen.[5] Many communities participate in "Purple Up" events throughout the year to recognize the military brat and their part in the military community. The events can include wearing purple T-shirts on specific days in April, including the campaign and upcoming events on websites, posting signs in schools and communities, providing resources for military children, and hosting programs specifically for military children.

In addition to purple, the dandelion is recognized as the flower of the military child. Like the dandelions, they move with the wind and bloom where they are planted, over and over again.

While the term brat has a negative connotation linked to it, the term military brat is anything but negative. It has been a term of endearment from the beginning, and over the years, military children have adopted military brat as their own within the military community and into adulthood.

Alongside their parents, military brats endure frequent moves, academic disruptions, and periods of separation from their parents (and extended family) while living in locations around the world. The military brat leads a life quite different from that of other children in the U.S. Each military child endures and comes to terms with their life as a military brat in their own way and at their own pace. How they feel about the term is as individual as they are. When asked about the term *military brat*, here is what they had to say.

Naomi M., 10
Daughter of a U.S. Air Force Mom:
I don't really like being called a military brat; I don't like being called a brat. I don't know why people call us that.

Emma S., 13
Daughter of a U.S. Air Force Mom:
I like it, being a military brat. I think people show you respect as a military brat.

Maddison S., 13
Daughter of a U.S. Coast Guard Mom:
I have never heard of military brats before, but I like being a military kid.

Maddie S., 14
Daughter of a U.S. Air Force Mom:
I think it's pretty cool to have the Military Brat title.

Caleb C., 16
Son of U.S. Air Force Mom:
I have not been called a military brat, just a military kid.

Alexis Q., 29
Daughter of a U.S. Air Force Mom:
I didn't mind being called a military brat; that is how I usually refer to myself when people ask me about where I'm from, because it's easier to understand that I have lived in multiple places.

Jamal Q, 30
Son of a U.S. Air Force Mom:
I don't mind being called a military brat. I don't view it as negative. That is what I call myself and my friends with military parents all the time. I don't see it as a negative thing because I get where it comes from. Brat always sounded funny to me, but it's just a way of recognizing military kids. I think some military kids were really brats. Sometimes, they would want to have more privileges because their parents had a higher rank, which led to them acting like brats. That definitely happens.

Walker S., 30

Son of a U.S. Air Force Mom:

I think being called a military brat gives me a weird, weird amount of pride. When talking to a friend, he said that I was not like other military brats, and when I asked why, he talked about a negative connotation with the term, military brat, for those who acted like they, instead of their parents, served. That's not me.

Myia E., 33

Daughter of a U.S. Air Force Mom

About being called a military brat, it depends on the person saying it because a lot of military brats get a bad rap, so people like to emphasize the 'brat' part. I mean, I've seen both sides of the coin, right? Of course, like seeing it through other people's perspective, yeah, there are some bratty military brats, so it can be a bit of a bad reputation. But now that I'm older, I embrace it; it's fine. I mean, what else am I going to call myself?

Jennifer V., 38

Daughter of a U.S. Air Force Mom:

I like being called a military brat; I don't mind. I don't have any negative feelings about it. It's just what we are; it's an exclusive club.

Chapter 3:

A CHILD'S PERSPECTIVE ON THEIR MOTHER'S SERVICE

"I'm a military baby, and it makes me proud to know that I'm the child of two parents that served our country. I feel very connected to our country, and I'm honored to be an American."[6]

—Ciara

Most of the time it is years before we, as parents, truly understand what our children think about our military service. What a young child feels can change significantly by the time they are teenagers, and again when they become adults. Not only will their age and level of maturity affect their understanding of their mom's service, but their experiences will also shape their opinions. Similarly, their mother's attitude toward her own service impacts how her children see military life.

While very young, military brats may not fully grasp what their moms do. Like any child of a working parent, they see their mom go off to work in the morning and come home in the evening. What happens in between is a mystery. The most crucial part is that she returns to comfort them, feed them, and tuck them into bed. If their needs are taken care of, their little minds don't know or care about what is happening outside their little bubbles. And in that, her uniform becomes an integral part of who she is rather than just what she does, and is just part of Mom, like her favorite coffee mug or the sound of her voice greeting them when she walks through the door.

When military children are a little older, they begin to notice things. They see the camo jacket, the boots by the door, the early mornings, and the late nights. They stand beside Mom during the Star-Spangled Banner, imitating her salute, long before they understand why.

During military exercises and field days, they wake up to find Mom gone or they get ready for bed and she is not home. Sometimes, they may not see her for a couple of days. It disrupts their day-to-day life, and they may not understand why. They only know that they see her less; they do not understand the importance of the training, which is necessary to keep our nation and our allies safe.

They may not know the details of military readiness, TDYs, or deployment rotations, but they know what absence feels like. The questions begin: "Why do you have to go?" "When will you be back?" Separation is part of military life, but for children, it's personal. Having their mom leave for days, weeks, or months requires an adjustment, and these separations can be stressful for their little minds. It's not about protecting freedom; it's about missing Mom. How they handle these separations can often depend on how their moms, families, and military 'village' help them understand and adjust. For many young military brats, these separations are a part of their military lifestyle and, hopefully, become easier to endure.

By the time military children reach their preteen and teenage years, they begin to understand more about what it means to be in the Armed Forces and their parents' commitment to serving. They can understand the symbol of the uniform and what it means to serve. They began to realize that wearing the uniform is more than a job, it really is a way of life, for us and our families. It is the symbol of our nation's strength and what we are willing to do to keep our nation safe. Military brats see the pre-dawn workouts, long hours, and time away from family. They see the toll the work takes on their mom's body and mind, but they also see pride in her eyes when she wears her uniform. They see civilian parents sacrificing their own careers, friendships, and closeness to family. They began to understand that wearing the uniform is not just a job, it is a sacrifice, a commitment to service, and to the United States. They begin to understand the seriousness of service in the Armed Forces.

Once military brats reach adulthood, I think they can truly understand and appreciate their parent's service. They realize that serving in the Armed Forces isn't just a job, it's a calling. Whether their feelings about their parent's service is good, bad, or indifferent, this is when they will be able to reflect on their own lives growing up and fully see the impact of their mom's service and the military lifestyle on their own lives and their future. Some will reflect with pride, knowing they were part of something larger than themselves. Others may carry scars from the sacrifices they made. Most will hold a mix of both—the good and the bad—woven together.

In the end, it is not just any one thing but all of the things that come with military service that will influence what our children think of our choice to serve in the Armed Forces. In truth, there is no single answer to how military children feel about their mother's service. If you ask a hundred military brats, you'll hear a hundred different stories. While they all live the same lifestyle, what they experience and what they take from it will be as unique as they are. That's why I asked the ones I could. I asked military brats of all ages to tell me how they feel about their mom's service in the Armed Forces. Here's what they had to say.

Zoe B., 8

Daughter of a U.S. Coast Guard Mom:

I didn't really know what she did, but I did know that my mom was in the Coast Guard. Well, I think it'd be hard. I believe she had something to do with the law. It was a lot of days of not really seeing her, but it's fun to ask her about all the things she did.

Blair S., 8

Son of a U.S. Coast Guard Mom:

My mom is in the Coast Guard, and I think she is an assistant superintendent. Sometimes, it's annoying because some events cause her to miss some of my important events, like baseball games and other things.

Aniya Y., 8

Daughter of a U.S. Navy Mom:

My mom is in the Navy. It's good, and she works very hard, and it's important.

Naomi M., 10

Daughter of a U.S. Air Force Mom:

My mom was in the Air Force; she was a personnelist. I am not sure what she did. It was hard. I didn't really like it because I didn't see her so much.

Emma S., 13

Daughter of a U.S. Air Force Mom:

I am not sure what my mom did. She was where people worked out sometimes. I think it's pretty cool that my mom served. I like that she helps people.

Maddison S., 13

Daughter of a U.S. Coast Guard Mom:

My mom is an Assistant Superintendent at the Coast Guard Academy. But her main job is Search & Rescue on the water.

Yeah, I feel it's cool and I'm really proud of my mom. I don't really know how to explain it, but it just feels good, knowing what she does. I think her job is really cool, but at the same time, I feel like there are a bunch of sacrifices I have to make that other kids don't.

Khloe B., 13

Daughter of a U.S. Air Force Mom:

My mom is in the Air Force; she is a nurse practitioner. I think that it's an honor to have a mom like her. Her family did not grow up with a lot of things. Her dad was in the Navy, and he was away a lot. He was always home for Christmas and other special occasions.

Hearing her stories makes me realize how much people in the Armed Forces have to sacrifice for their families. My mom deployed to Afghanistan a few months after I was born. She kept journals about her life there and later shared them with me. I think she was gone for at least seven months. She missed so much; my dad recorded a lot for her, but she missed out on a lot. When she came home, I didn't recognize her, and I clung to my dad, hiding behind his legs. That experience made her sad because her daughter didn't know who she was.

Maddie S., 14

Daughter of a U.S. Air Force Mom:

My mom is in the Air Force. She is a manager of the DFAC (a dining facility). She also works in lodging and fitness. I think it's pretty cool. I think it's pretty cool because she did a lot of stuff.

Atiya J., 16

Daughter of a U.S. Navy Mom:

I was four when my mom joined the Navy. She is an air traffic controller. It's a good thing; I know how important her job is.

Caleb C., 16

Son of U.S. Air Force Mom:

My mom oversees a bunch of nurses in the Learning and Development workforce. I think it's pretty cool that she's a major and all the cool stuff she does. I think it's pretty cool that she is in the military.

D'Aaron C., 23

Son of U.S. Air National Guard Mom:

The military lifestyle has had an impact on our family in many ways, both positive and negative, but overall, I would say positive.

My mom is an officer in the Air National Guard; I am not sure exactly what she does, but she does a lot of things. I am very, very proud of her, and I love what she does.

The military is a part-time job for her. She joined because she knew she had to provide for her family. So, two jobs were the way to go. The military was open, and it was perfect for her at the time.

Alexis Q., 29

Daughter of a U.S. Air Force Mom:

My mom served in the Air Force, and I was never really sure what she did for work because I was young. I don't think her being in the military was really much different from nonmilitary families.

Megan T, 28

Daughter of a U.S. Air Force Mom:

My mom was in the Air Force, so was my dad and my stepdad. I had to ask my mom what she did because I didn't know, but she was an information manager and later, a resource advisor.

I think she was such a badass, and I still believe that. My parents got divorced when I was pretty young, so it was just my mom and me. And I remember when she had to do an early morning shift and put the flag out. It would be like her waking me up at 5:00 in the morning, and I'd go into the office with her. I always liked every office she ever worked in. There was always a ton of snacks. I'm pretty sure I ate a lot of snacks in my day.

She instilled in me the work ethic I have because I was around her so much when she worked at AETC (Air Education and Training Command), at Randolph Air Force Base. Her office was close to the youth center, and she worked so hard; she'd say, "All right, well, you can just walk over from the youth center from here."

She was just very dedicated to her job, and even at a young age, I could tell from her coworkers or the people around her that she was highly regarded.

I definitely would not have the work ethic I have today if it weren't for her. So, I definitely think it was just a really cool experience and then getting to brag about her when I'm older and when people are like, "Oh, your mom is in the military?" and I can say, "Yeah, she was in for twenty-two years."

Jamal Q, 30
Son of a U.S. Air Force Mom:
My mom was in the Air Force, and she was a paralegal and then a first sergeant. As I got older, I recognized the importance and sacrifice that goes along with military service. I think it was always really cool seeing how much respect and appreciation she and my dad would get when we went to places and people learned that they both served.

My mom and dad did a good job of spending time with us, taking vacations, and visiting places. But when I was younger, I definitely remember times when it seemed unfair. It was just taking time away from us and preventing us from spending time with my mom. There was anger, or a sense of unfairness, about having to share her with people because it didn't make sense to me.

There were many benefits for me and a lot of sacrifices that my mom made. I recognize that now that I have a job. I understand it more.

Walker S., 30
Son of a U.S. Air Force Mom:
My mom and my dad were in the Air Force. I think my mom joined when I was about six years old. She started out as a behavioral scientist, transitioned into protocol, and later became a psychologist.

Oh my gosh, she has met so many cool people. She has always been my hero. It was pretty cool for me to be out with her in uniform and all these people thanking her for her service and calling her a hero.

My granddad was a hippie and very anti-cop and anti-military. But when my mom joined, my grandad could not have been prouder. My mom was also a rebel. She had me at nineteen and pretty much raised me by herself. It was huge for me to see her going into the military, especially since it was right around 9/11 (coordinated terrorist suicide attacks against the U.S. in 2001). I think the world of my mom's service. It not only opened doors for her, but it also helped her out of a tight spot.

Looking back, my mom's joining had more of a self-serving purpose and in a very net positive way. I don't think anybody should have to join the military, but I respect that it's what my mom did. Especially as a woman, a single mom at the time, that's really, really inspiring to me. My mom was a superhero to me, and she still is.

Myia E., 33
Daughter of a U.S. Air Force Mom
My mom was in the Air Force, and for the most part, she was a hospital administrator. I know she specialized in IT here and there, but her main job was hospital administrator.

I think she did a great job in the Air Force. You know, I mean, with her circumstances, the military was a good move. I didn't think she would be in for as long as she did, but I like to think that her joining, and her service made a difference and a positive impact on other people. Living a military lifestyle is definitely a completely different life from what many nonmilitary people would think.

Jennifer V., 38

Daughter of a U.S. Air Force Mom:

My mom served in the Air Force, and she had a lot of jobs. The one I remember the most is when she was an MTM (Military Training Manager). I don't know why I remember that title; I don't even know what the job was, but I remember it. She was also a law office manager and then a first sergeant.

Having my parents serve was all I ever knew. I did think it was pretty cool because both of my parents were in the military. I didn't have very many friends whose moms were in the military. And I don't think I had any friends with only their mom in the military. It just seemed like for most people, their dad was in the military, but my mom was too.

People say that many things help keep our country the way it is. But having a mom who is a part of that, there's just a sense of pride that comes with that and, like, a sense of purpose.

Chapter 4:
LIVING THE MILITARY LIFESTYLE

> "Being a military kid is full of challenges, but on the other end of all those challenges is the great feeling of knowing that you have made sacrifices for your country, however big or small those sacrifices may have been."[7]
>
> — Ryan Patrick Curtin, 2014 Navy Military Child of the Year

When people think about the military lifestyle, they usually think it entails frequent moves and deployment. It does, and they are probably the most common aspects that people not affiliated with the military will identify with the military. But life in the military is more than that. It's waking up on base to the sound of Reveille heard across the installation. It's hearing the Star-Spangled Banner so often that the tune is a part of your childhood. It's growing up in a community where everyone understands the same unspoken rules because they're living them too.

It is a lifestyle that offers a child the opportunity to travel and learn about various locations (both nationally and internationally), cultures, and people. Even if they don't move frequently, they still get the chance to meet and experience new people, learning about diverse backgrounds and cultures from those on the installations where their mom is serving.

Most military installations can be self-contained and offer m any amenities that you find in a small city or town, including a school system, daycare centers, grocery store, gas stations, a theater, fitness centers, restaurants, medical facilities, police stations, veterinarians, pools, parks, libraries, clubs, a law office, housing, a place to take college courses, and even a department store.

The installation's setup makes it easy for military members and their families to find a sense of familiarity when moving from one installation to the next in the United States or abroad. I spoke with one mom who recalled some apprehension when moving with her bi-racial children to a military installation in a Southern state; but she found that the military community, at the new location, was just as open and welcoming as the one they'd left behind.

Most military installations in the U.S. and overseas offer schools for military children. These schools are run very much like most other public schools but with one big difference: every student there knows what it's like to be part of a military family. They provide the same opportunities and classes that you would find in your typical school, like band, sports, student council, AP classes, and field trips. Another benefit of these schools is that most classes are relatively small, offering a lower student-to-teacher ratio. For example, my oldest daughter's graduation class at Edgren High School at Misawa Air Base, Japan was just over fifty students, while my younger children's graduation classes at Steele High School in Cibolo, Texas numbered just under five hundred for each graduation.

Not everyone will choose this option, but many do, especially in locations where English is not the first language. In these schools, military children are likely to meet people from all parts of the U. S. and around the globe. Children who, like them, are military brats. These schools can provide a sense of familiarity and belonging. They offer the chance to settle in, surrounded by other young people who share their military lifestyle and can relate to 'being the new kid.'

In addition to schools, most military installations provide youth centers for military children. These centers offer not only a place for kids to go to after school but also provide organized sports, trips, and other activities. Whether it's soccer, football, overnight lock-ins, snacks, or tutoring help, the youth center is a staple for many military moms of elementary school–aged children. Like schools on military installations, youth centers also offer the opportunity to meet and socialize while also providing a better understanding of other cultures.

Life in the military community offers the opportunity to meet and interact with people who don't necessarily look like them. On a military installation, they will meet peers whose parents are from various backgrounds and ethnic groups. I have worked with people from all over the world who serve in or work with our Armed Forces, and many of them have spouses and children. This helps our children to be open to the world. To embrace difference instead of fearing it.

My oldest was born in Spain, and her daycare provider, who was my co-worker's wife, was Spanish. Having a Spanish daycare provider meant that, for eight to ten hours a day, my daughter was immersed in another culture, not just observing it but living it. We also lived in a Spanish neighborhood where we were the only Americans, and for many of the children there, my daughter was the first Black child they had ever interacted with up close. The lessons she learned about acceptance and cultural differences started early, and they stayed with her.

While the military provides many unique experiences for military children, it comes with expectations as well. Some of these could be as simple as knowing how to behave during the Retreat and the playing of the Star-Spangled Banner or living overseas and learning to follow the customs of the community outside the installation.

Others are heavier, like knowing that if you misbehave, it might not just be a personal consequence; serious offenses could affect their parents' careers. Military brats, like the rest of the military community, are expected to follow the general rules and guidelines of behavior while on military installations and in overseas locations, both on and off the installation. For example, growing up on an installation means you will stop and stand silently during the Star-Spangled Banner, it means carrying issued military identification cards, respecting curfews, knowing and respecting local laws and customs when overseas, and it means that your parents can be required to report to their commanding officer to address your misconduct.

For me, serving in the Armed Forces was the best decision my husband and I could have made, not just for ourselves, but for our family. It gave us experiences we might not have had otherwise. But I know that is just my perspective. So, I asked some military brats—those who lived this life from the inside—what they thought about growing up in the military. Here's what they shared.

Zoe B., 8
Daughter of a U.S. Coast Guard Mom:
Well, I think it'd be pretty hard. And you wouldn't usually get to see your family a lot because you would be moving around a lot to different places.

Blair S., 8
Son of U.S. Coast Guard Mom:
I think it's nice because I get to go to events, and I get to go to the Exchange where I can buy stuff. I can go to my mom's office and get free candy.

Aniya Y., 8
Daughter of a U.S. Navy Mom:
It's all I know; this is normal for me. I like it.

Naomi M., 10
Daughter of a U.S. Air Force Mom:
I know it's pretty cool to be in the military. I think it's fun, and I like moving. I like the perks of being able to go on base. My favorite move was to Germany.

I am not really close to my relatives, and I didn't get to see them that often. I don't know half the cousins my mom talks about.

Maddison S., 13
Daughter of a U.S. Coast Guard Mom:
It can be hard sometimes, but also, like, really fun.

I feel like it's really cool because I, personally, get to meet new people, see new things, and do other things that most kids wouldn't be able to do. I feel that having someone in the military allows me to learn new things and meet really nice people.

Khloe B., 13
Daughter of a U.S. Air Force Mom:
Both my parents are in the military, and it can be hard for everyone.

We lived in Maryland for four years. I attended a regular school, and I really felt like I was just another citizen in that state who wasn't going to move any time soon. Even though I knew, in the back of my head, that I would have to leave in four years, my classmates were shocked by my move. But I knew I would have to move.

Maddie S., 14
Daughter of a U.S. Air Force Mom:
It's hard because you didn't get to choose whether you wanted to be a part of it. You have to live the lifestyle.

Even though we didn't live on base, it was cool to be able to go to the base and do stuff. I had my own ID (military identification) card, and that was pretty cool. And the healthcare was excellent.

Atiya J., 16
Daughter of a U.S. Navy Mom:
I get to do a lot more stuff than other kids. I feel like I have more responsibilities. I think it's what I am used to.

Caleb C., 16
Son of U.S. Air Force Mom:
I guess the main thing everyone looks at is moving every two and a half to three years. Also, being an only child is fifty-fifty; sometimes it is great, and sometimes it is not.

Military moms work long hours, so there are times when you may not see them. They could be on-call all the time, or they could be at work a lot. They do work a lot, so I think it's very intense for the mom and the kid.

I'm used to it. My mom only had me, and maybe I'm used to being on my own when she's at work. Back then, with all the babysitters, it wasn't great.

It can be rough, but I don't think I would want it any other way.

D'Aaron C., 21
Son of a U.S. Air National Guard Mom:
If you had asked me that question ten years ago, I would have said I hate everything about it, and I wish she had never joined. But you ask me this question now, and I understand her service better.

You know, she's had to go away for extended periods. That makes it rough, but it also helped me become a stronger individual, and I had to learn to do many things. I have learned from my mom's service, and I've learned from her strength and perseverance.

I was just blessed to have good people around me. I have an excellent support system with understanding and caring people that I can talk to, you know, when times get rough. Even when I was younger, it was the same because I had my brother with me.

Alexis Q., 29
Daughter of a U.S. Air Force Mom:
I think the military lifestyle is pretty nice. I definitely miss some of the benefits. I had some experiences that most of my current friends didn't have.

Megan T, 28
Daughter of a U.S. Air Force Mom:
I think there are two things. I felt very privileged; privileged to have a free gym to go to, or the commissary, and have everything be tax-free. And even at Randolph (Air Force Base), we had such a niche group of individuals, of kids whose parents were in the military. They moved around. We have just a better understanding of what we're all going through. So, I loved my time being on base.

I don't, and this is probably just specific to Randolph, but my public education before Randolph was a pretty big struggle for me to adjust to at school. At Randolph, it was just so much easier, and I think I excelled there. But I remember it being pretty easy because I was so young, and that was the first time I had ever experienced other military kids in school, because the school I went to in Clovis (New Mexico) didn't have a lot of military kids. I thought it was like a great transition. I don't really remember it being hard because my mom also put me in the youth center right away. So, they were the kids I was hanging out with in the summer too. It was fun.

I think going to school on base offered smaller classes, and the things I heard about happening at the local high school were unheard of at Randolph. Maybe because we were a smaller group of kids and our parents had eyes on us all the time.

Also, there were also points where it was so sheltered that when I got to college, I was around nonmilitary people, civilians, and I know I'm a civilian, but it was like a huge shock to my world. Even realizing that gyms weren't free and that was just something I had grown up with, it was a tough transition going into college. I found some people don't have structure (of the military lifestyle) in their lives.

It was also a really hard transition when my (military) ID was taken away. Like, "I can't go on base anymore?"

Jamal Q, 30
Son of a U.S. Air Force Mom:
I don't think I have ever hated living the military lifestyle. It was a lot, but I enjoyed being able to move around. I think it gave me a broader sense of community. I had a wider circle of people I could depend on when my parents were on call, had to go TDY, or deploy.

There were times when I spent time with my friends' parents. At their house, I never felt like I was left with strangers. You form a tight-knit group. It was like everyone knew each other; kind of like being raised in a big family. These people could easily step in; it was like adults I could respect and trust.

The military lifestyle has afforded me numerous opportunities to travel to see places outside the United States. It was normal for me, and it is a bit of a shock when I meet people who have never been outside their city or state. It is also about experiencing new things and trying different things, which is something that I've gotten from the military, specifically from being a military brat. I think that is something that a lot of people don't have.

Living on base was cool and gave me access to a lot of things. And even when I lived off base, I found a group of friends who were also military kids, and that made it super easy to become friends and connect with people. I'd say finding your tribe, community ... your personal group is important.

Walker S., 30
Son of a U.S. Air Force Mom:
While I was growing up, the best thing about it was that I always had friends in different locations. I can't go to a state where I don't know somebody from my travels. I am still friends with a lot of the military kids I knew growing up.

I was basically a latchkey kid growing up. I have a bunch of half-siblings from my bio dad, so I'm in touch with a lot of them now, but there is a considerable age disparity. I grew up as an only child functionally. Now my mom's like, "I've messed you up, or I could have, I am so sorry." And I'm like, "I feel normal and I'm pretty well adjusted."

I. 100 percent. still consider myself a military brat. I can't take away that part of me that grew up that way. It's an integral part of my personality. I think it's a huge reason why my career has been successful and why I've fought for promotions, raises, and other opportunities.

Myia E., 33
Daughter of a U.S. Air Force Mom
Mostly, the military lifestyle sucked because I am my mom's only child. Growing up like this is all I know, and we had to keep moving and stuff. So, like at one point, when I was a kid, I was like, "Can we, like, stay in one location long enough so that I might go to the same school for a few years? Because I don't want to keep trying to fit in."

However, I mean there are pros to that too, because when you constantly move around and you're meeting all kinds of people, it brings out that extroverted side of you, right? You have to learn how to communicate with strangers, and you learn how to make new friends as you go along. Because some people know the same people their whole life, they don't know anything outside that circle.

It definitely broadens your mindset, especially when it comes to how the world operates, because you're seeing pieces of the culture from different parts of the United States or the world, right? So that was cool.

Unfortunately, being an only child, you tend to feel lonely a lot of the time. However, it was easier for me to understand myself, my own person, after going through all of that. So, there's, I mean, there's pros and cons to both sides, right?

Jennifer V., 38
Daughter of a U.S. Air Force Mom:
The military lifestyle is just how we lived. But I do think it made a difference that we usually lived on base. So, everyone that I went to school with, everyone that I knew, experienced the same thing. So, it's different because you all already know that everybody lives this lifestyle. So, it's like you don't feel singled out. Because we're all sharing the same experience.

That's a lot different from, say, the school where I work. We do get some military kids there, but not a lot. The general population of students really does not understand. They are like, "Why are you here? Why did you move here in the middle of junior year?"

So, I think just having a group of people around me who understood what it was like and who could be empathetic really helped make it easier than it could have been if I had been placed in, I don't know, some other school. Like, if my parents retired and we just moved to the middle of nowhere with no military ties. I think that would have been a lot harder.

Chapter 5:
WE'RE MOVING AGAIN

"If you're brave enough to say goodbye, life will reward you with a new hello."[8]

—Paulo Coelho

Many children move only once or twice during their childhood. Military brats move so often that it becomes part of who they are. For them, packing up and starting over isn't the exception. It's the rule. Some military brats move five, ten, even fifteen times before high school graduation. Some start moving before they even know their own address. Moving can be as much a part of the military lifestyle as wearing a uniform, following the chain of command, and enduring deployments, all of which fall under the category of "going where you are needed." Still, for military brats, it is often called "another goodbye."

Packing up the family and moving equals change, and change is not something that comes easily for many of us. It can be full of uncertainty and fear of the unknown, and it can be even more daunting for children.

As a mom, I understood this in a way many people might not. Growing up, my own family moved frequently, not because of military orders, but because life took us from place to place. I never stayed in the same school for more than three years. These moves were not always welcome; they were just a part of my life as I grew up. There seemed always to be a new home, a new school, and new friends.

As a military mom, people often asked me, "Was your dad in the military too?"

My answer was always, "No, but it sure felt like it."

So, when my husband and I were raising our children in the Air Force, I could empathize with the difficulty of changing schools, leaving friends, and starting over. Even if I understood it, that didn't make it easier for them.

Just as it wasn't always easy for me as a child, moving wasn't always easy for my children. I remember my oldest daughter pleading to stay in South Carolina when we received orders to Japan. She had finally found her place, made close friends, and didn't want to leave. Her friend even asked if my daughter could live with them instead. They presented the idea with all the seriousness that only a preteen can summon.

For my youngest, the most challenging part wasn't leaving; it was watching her best friend move away. Military brats don't just leave. Sometimes, they have to say goodbye to their best friend or newest teammate.

As parents, we have a better understanding of the necessity of relocating from one military installation to another. We also know what awaits us at the new location. In the Air Force, before a move, members are usually assigned a sponsor to help them acclimate to the new location. With every move, I would quickly meet someone who knew a friend, a co-worker, or a supervisor from past assignments, again making the move much easier.

But for a child, a decision is made without their input, a choice that changes their whole world overnight. To them, it's just packing up and moving yet again, which causes frustration and even anxiety. Sometimes, the stress of moving shows up in unexpected ways: acting out, withdrawal, or unfinished schoolwork. Other times, it sparks resilience, courage, and an adventurous spirit that stays with them for life.

Through the years, I learned that preparation and attitude make all the difference. We involved our kids in the process early. My husband and I tried to tell the kids about the move as soon as we knew about it to give them as much time as possible to prepare, both consciously and unconsciously. We also tried to model optimism for each move. Even if I wasn't looking forward to the move, I wanted my children to get excited and ready for it. It wasn't always easy. It could be as simple as discussing the new location or learning about attractions that the kids might enjoy once we arrive.

For me, one assignment that was easy to prepare for was to a base in northern Japan; I was excited about living in another country again, and I have always found Asian culture fascinating. Reading about Japanese culture and trying to learn the language was both exciting and fun. Before we went to Japan, we knew a little about the culture and the area around the base we were being stationed. We started learning about the area and everyone was excited about the move and the places we might want to visit, like Akihabara, the bullet train, and Disney Tokyo. Once we got there, we found even more things to learn and do, including trying all the Japanese cuisine, festivals, and the public hot baths.

On the other hand, our assignment to Sumter, South Carolina, was not so exciting. Still, we managed to find nearby places to visit, the local shopping, and nearby installations we could visit, parks to experience, and family to visit. Our time in South Carolina even overlapped with my sister's assignment to the same installation and coincided with our extended family's planned vacation at nearby Myrtle Beach.

No matter the amount of preparation, it can still be scary trading the known for the unknown. The service members will know where they are going and what they will be doing. You have the continuity of your work to depend on; you will likely be doing the same thing or something similar. This familiarity makes it easier to settle into your new assignment. Our families, and especially our kids, don't always have that comfort. Each move is new and can bring on new apprehensions that go along with a new home, a new school, and no friends.

While moving can be hard on a child, it can be even harder for a teenager. Even though today's technology can make moving, staying in touch, and maintaining friendships easier, relocating is still hard on so many levels for so many reasons. This can be the time when kids start developing relationships and finding their best friend and maybe their first love. They're fighting desperately to establish their identities in their own groups, as their bodies change in strange and uncomfortable ways. And, of course, there's that rebellious phase that makes them want to do the opposite of anything their parents say. Adding a relocation into the mix is like kicking a hormone-fueled wasp nest.

When thinking about military kids faced with relocation, I am reminded of episode three of season two of *Star Trek: Deep Space Nine*, where family members have to evacuate. In this episode, the commander's son, Jake, says, "Just when I thought I found a new home and a new friend, I have to leave again." That captures it perfectly.

But moving also has its rewards. Experiencing the various cities, states, and countries enriches their childhoods on many levels. It broadens our children's horizons and exposes them to ideas and cultures that can help them become better citizens and adults. It means meeting new people from all over the world and developing new friendships that can last a lifetime.

Enduring moves as a child can help develop stronger social skills. Whether it is making new friends, meeting new teachers, or fitting into new communities, these experiences make for stronger social skills. Most military brats become adept at adjusting to different social situations. Even if they don't enjoy it, this is a skill that they carry with them into adulthood.

For many military brats, moving awakens a desire to travel and see new parts of the world. It can instill a sense of self and resilience that helps them fit in wherever they are, not just in childhood but into adulthood.

Relocating from one installation to another can play a significant role in helping military brats develop the ability to adapt to change. Through the process of moving, they learn what it means to leave behind the familiar and face new environments, people, and experiences. This skill becomes especially important as they experience major transitions later in life, such as leaving home for college, starting a new job, or even making a career shift. Although the ability to accept and embrace change may not come naturally or immediately, the challenges and experiences of frequent relocations will prepare them over time. As adults, they are often better equipped to handle the many instances of change, drawing on the resilience and flexibility they developed during their childhood moves.

So, what do military brats say about moving again and again? I asked them, and here's what they shared.

Zoe B., 8
Daughter of a U.S. Coast Guard Mom:
Well. It was stressful because you leave a friend, then you make new friends, then you move again, and so forth.

Blair S., 8
Son of U.S. Coast Guard Mom:
I have only moved three times in my mom's career. I think it's annoying because I had to leave my old house a lot, and I could hang out with my friend in the backyard, where we look for treasures. I have made a new friend. I like to hang out with him a lot, but I mostly have to go to his house because we live at the Coast Guard Academy.

Aniya Y., 8
Daughter of a U.S. Navy Mom:
We've moved, but I don't remember it.

Naomi M., 10
Daughter of a U.S. Air Force Mom:
We have moved three times. I like moving, meeting new people, and seeing different places. That was fun. Living in another country was fun, and It's a very beautiful place. Not many people here could say, "I lived there."

Emma S., 13
Daughter of a U.S. Air Force Mom:
We were at four bases. Moving is all right. It is like a new exploration, new places, even if it's Georgia. And, sometimes, we would get new furniture.

Maddison S., 13
Daughter of a U.S. Coast Guard Mom:
I have moved five times, and sometimes I really like moving. But sometimes I feel like the hardest part about being like my mom's daughter and what she does is the moving because that's my least favorite thing.

I usually don't like it when it happens, but then once we get to the new place, I always love it. There hasn't been a place where I've regretted living.

Khloe B., 13
Daughter of a U.S. Air Force Mom:
We have moved four times, which, compared to other people (in the military), is not a lot, not even in the slightest. So, I'm kind of grateful for that.

My last move was tough. It was right after COVID (coronavirus disease of 2019), and I had already felt like I had to reintroduce myself at school. COVID had already put us in a different place; we were locked in at home and didn't have the everyday human interactions. And finally, we were able to be around people wearing masks. That really made me appreciate human interaction; we are not supposed to be alone for long periods. Then it was time to move.

And that's why I probably got so emotional the day we had to move. It was just a few days before summer break. I had just had my fifth-grade graduation, and I was having most of the people in my class sign my yearbook and stuff.

When we got in the car, and I opened my yearbook, I started crying and crying the whole ride home. I was saying how I hated the military and how I wished that I could be somebody else. I was also saying how I hated that she was in the military, and if she wasn't, we could just live a normal life.

I know that hurt her. I think for me, at my age, a lot was going on. You know, you're developing more, you are gaining a sense of independence, but also a sense of belonging, and then boom, you have to move. So, it can be hard.

My mom was a military child, and she had to go to, I think, eleven different schools. That must have been very hard, having to restart your life over and over again.

Maddie S., 15
Daughter of a U.S. Air Force Mom:
We PCS'd three times but moved nine times. You get to see new places but moving wasn't always fun. For the moves, we spent a lot of time in cars, and I didn't have a phone. That was hard, but I always made friends easily.

Atiya J., 16
Daughter of a U.S. Navy Mom:
I have only moved twice. With the last move, it was okay because we did distance learning and everything was at home. But after that was over, and I finally got to school, I had to find new friends.

Caleb C., 16
Son of a U.S. Air Force Mom:
I don't remember much of moving; I think we moved twice. The major one I remember was when we moved to Vegas (Los Vegas, Nevada). We were there for three years, and then we moved back here.

I think we were supposed to move one more time, but my mom put in the work and worked it out so we could stay here.

D'Aaron C., 21
Son of a U.S. Air National Guard Mom:
We moved about four times, I think. I've been blessed to have met some of the greatest friends I've ever had, and I'm still really good friends with them today.

Moving has helped me learn a lot. It helped me learn, at some point, how to be by myself, but it also helped me learn how to appreciate family more and helped me learn how to appreciate and enjoy those I have around me, because you never really know when the next move is coming.

Growing up, I thought I was shy and reserved, but I was not. It's just the fact that I was nervous and anxious. I had to meet new people everywhere I went.

Alexis Q., 29
Daughter of a U.S. Air Force Mom:
After I was born, we moved maybe four or five times. It's always strange to be the new kid in school, but I always enjoyed traveling.

These days, I don't really picture myself in one place too, too long, even without the military lifestyle.

Megan T, 28
Daughter of a U.S. Air Force Mom:
I actually only moved twice with my mom. I was born in Clovis, New Mexico, at Cannon Air Force Base. We stayed there until I was probably eight or nine, and then we moved to Randolph Air Force Base. That is where I have been ever since. I was living with my dad when my parents got divorced; my mom was already in San Antonio, so I moved over with her later. But I think I started second grade or third grade at Randolph.

Sometimes I feel grateful that I didn't have to move, but I'm not sure. As I got older, my friend Jamie and her family moved every single year. They didn't stay anywhere, I don't think, for more than two years. We've been friends since the eighth grade, and I believe her family PCS'd to Washington, District of Columbia (D.C.), Idaho, Colorado, and Wyoming. Every time I went to visit, you know, Jamie's dad gave me so many opportunities. I even got to go through the facility at Cheyenne Mountain after I got my security clearance.

Jamal Q, 30

Son of a U.S. Air Force Mom:

We lived in Japan for seven years and then moved twice while in Texas. I don't remember our moves before that.

We moved, but I know people who moved more often. I don't feel like I had to go through that; it was more of my friends who moved away.

In this day and age, I think it is a lot easier for military kids to stay connected to their friends with social media and other digital tools. So, I imagine that's not a huge deal. I mean, it definitely sucks going to new schools and everything, but I think it's one of those things that when you're young, it sucks. But as you get into middle school, it's okay, and you learn that that's just sort of how it is, and you learn to appreciate the fact that you get to live in so many different places and meet so many people.

Walker S., 30

Son of a U.S. Air Force Mom:

If I am not mistaken, I think we did eight moves. Oh, it sucked. It wasn't very good. It was terrible.

The first move was from my hometown, a small town in central Illinois. My mom had always wanted to get out of there, and this was her way to get out. Even as a kid, that first move felt like it was needed. I don't know if that was influenced by my mom or the situation. But every move after that just got harder and harder. Especially the Randolph move, from Randolph (Air Force Base) to Washington, D.C. Going from the school at Randolph with two or three hundred students to a school with around twenty-five hundred kids was a culture shock to the ninth degree.

Every move was significantly harder, and at the time, I was very spiteful and jaded about it. But then, afterwards, looking back on it, I think it is the number one reason that I am a resilient human being when it comes to work and my personal life.

I have talked about it with my spouse, who doesn't come from a military family or background at all. Now, I talk, all the time, about how now I think it's essential to move, if or when we have children. I'm like, "We need one big move at a minimum because it changes you differently. It lets you see the world from a different lens." So, I guess I've flip-flopped completely.

Myia E., 33
Daughter of a U.S. Air Force Mom
We moved about six times, and my mom drove for a couple of moves when I was in college.

Well, I used to hate it, but now I'm just tired of it. However, it prepared me for doing road trips because of what we were going through. And, of course, I learned before I became an adult how to deal with movers and the entire moving process, including packing, moving, and unpacking.

It's so cool because sometimes when we move, we would make like pit stops, you know, to see family members we haven't seen in a while or visit friends or something. Sometimes we would stop somewhere we hadn't been before. So, you get a free "adventure" while you're moving.

However, it can quickly get pretty tiring during those road trips, depending on their length. One of our longest rides was from Idaho to here in Maryland. She took the brunt of it, of course, by doing the driving. I couldn't help my mom drive until I was fifteen or sixteen. It's just one of those things. Of course, I had plenty of books to read and games to play. You know, and I had my portable DVD (digital versatile disc) player back in the day.

Now, I know I could do it, but do I want to keep doing this? I'm really tired of moving at this point.

Jennifer V., 38
Daughter of a U.S. Air Force Mom:
I remember moving. I don't remember moving to Arizona, but I know we did. I don't remember moving to Texas. But I do remember moving into different houses in Texas. I remember moving to South Carolina. And I remember thinking it was not that big of a deal. And then I remember moving to Misawa (Air Base, Japan).

I think I have the most negative feelings about moving. But really, I can only remember one move that really upset me. I don't know if it was just because of my age, but it left some lasting impression. But it really wasn't that bad. It wasn't as bad as I thought it was going to be. I remember that I felt like it was significantly life changing. In the sixth grade, I just thought it was going to be the worst possible thing that could ever happen. I have to move to a new country, make new friends, and go back to elementary school.

Chapter 6:
WHILE YOU WERE GONE

"No matter how far away we are from each other in distance, or in time, when we look up into the clear night Sky. We will always see the same Moon."[9]

— Adam Stanley

Separation from family is part of military life. It starts from day one. Whether it's basic training, officer training school, TDY's, or deployment, there comes a time when every service member has to say goodbye. For military moms, these goodbyes can be especially difficult. Sometimes we're gone for days, sometimes months, and occasionally, we can be gone for a year or more if military needs dictate it.

We know it comes with the uniform and will happen throughout our career. We know it and we accept it. But our children? They only know that Mom is gone. While they may not always understand, they get used to seeing us pack up and take off. I am not sure it ever gets easy for them, but they come to accept these absences as a part of life.

When I had to leave, I always tried to prepare my kids. We talked about how long I would be away, and what they could expect while I was gone. I wanted them to see it as temporary, not permanent. I hoped it would be easier for them to see it as a temporary situation that would have an end.

When they are younger, military brats may not fully understand the circumstances around their mom's absence. They may miss their mom and the routine that revolves around her. All they know is that she is not there.

Although sometimes they might enjoy a break in routine and doing something different or spending time with extended family members. Sometimes, it can be fun having Mom away and just having time with Dad. It could mean eating out more, or a little more freedom, or a change of pace around the house. I know, for us, when my husband was away, it was always a little different around the house.

Sometimes, I would wish that time would stand still for them. That way, when I got back, nothing would have changed, and we could pick up where we left off. Unfortunately, that is not how it works, and when I was gone, their day-to-day lives did not come to a halt. They would adjust to my absence, and when I returned home, I would sometimes find that things had changed. Routines shift, children grow, and you come back to a world that feels both familiar and unfamiliar. Some changes were small, and some were big. Like when I was sent TDY right after PCS'ing, and in my absence, my husband had to select our housing without my input.

One mom I know returned from a deployment to find that her husband and children had created a new routine of preparing for bed, waking up on their own, and doing more around the house in her absence. There was no going back to the old normal. There was only adjusting to the new routine.

These absences became a part of our lives as military families. Looking back, I see that they helped my children develop a sense of resilience and even independence at an early age. Even today, I see the same 'nothing to it but to do it attitude' in each of them.

There are times that "when" you leave is just as impactful as "where" you are going. Leaving for a few days may not seem important, but for the child who is having a birthday or another significant event during your absence, it can be a huge deal.

On the other hand, having your mom leave for training or a conference is quite different than having her deploy. In the case of the latter, it can be scary for our children; this is especially true as they get older.

An older child can understand the circumstances of deployment and the potential dangers associated with it. In these cases, the child can spend time worrying about their mom.

These separations can affect children differently and manifest in various ways. For some, it leads to negative behavioral changes: slipping grades, acting out, or withdrawing. For others, it sparks a drive to excel, a way to gain control over something when everything else feels out of control. When community members who interact regularly with the child don't understand the possible frustrations of these separations, it can be even harder on the child.

Another form of absence can be remote assignments, and having your mom leave for a year or more can be unimaginable until it happens. Such a long separation is tough for the entire family and, sometimes, the extended family as well. When the mother is the primary caregiver and is absent for more than a year, the spouse and children must adjust. Sometimes that means getting help from family members or friends. For the children of single parents, it often means living with extended family, family friends, or others in their military community. Entering a completely different family unit for any amount of time is jarring as the surety of their home and schedule is left behind.

No matter how hard we try to prepare our children, these absences can cause sadness and even anger. We do our best to foresee and help them work through their feelings, to help them understand and find positive ways to deal with our absence. Like, making sure they have what they need for upcoming events during our absence, setting up times to call and chat about what's happening back home, or making sure we have a support system set up to help them deal with life while we are gone.

Sometimes, they manage to work through it all on their own, with their dads, siblings, or extended family or with their friends who are also military brats and can understand what they are going through. In the end, the important thing is that they find a way to work through it and find tools to help deal with it the next time it's necessary for mom to be away.

I have learned that for military brats, these separations are just another part of the military lifestyle. For most, it's the only life they know, and these separations are as normal as attending school, relocating to another installation, or saying goodbye to a classmate who is moving. Having a mom go TDY or deploy is a common experience. These periods of separations become just another part of who mom is.

Just because it's their normal doesn't mean it is easy. We hope our children learn that being part of something bigger than yourself sometimes comes with a cost, but also with rewards: resilience, courage, and the ability to adapt. As they get older, they begin to understand the necessity of why Mom will be gone for a while. They adjust to the separations. They might even take pride in what their mom is doing, and the sacrifices she is making.

When I spoke with military children about these experiences, here's what they shared.

Zoe B., 8
Daughter of a U.S. Coast Guard Mom:
Well. When my mom was gone, I missed her a lot, but we got to call each other. So, that was nice.

Blair S., 8
Son of U.S. Coast Guard Mom:
Sometimes, my mom can be gone for a few days. How do I handle that? It's sort of good because I get to play Fortnite because she barely lets me play on my PS5 (PlayStation 5). We get to eat out a lot, and I can do more stuff.

Aniya Y., 8
Daughter of a U.S. Navy Mom:
When she had to go away, it was hard. I was crying because I missed her, and then I was happy because it was almost time for her to come back. When I was sad, I could call her, and I got ice cream. When she came back, I could hang out with her again.

Naomi M., 10
Daughter of a U.S. Air Force Mom:
When my mom was gone, it would get very hard. We missed her, but we knew she was coming back. Our dad would put a picture on the wall we had, and that was her. I also think there was like a vase or something, and we had marbles, and we put a marble in each day for when she was away. That helped a lot.

Emma S., 13
Daughter of a U.S. Air Force Mom:
I don't remember her deployment, but when my mom was away TDY, I was kind of sad and angry, but it was okay because I had my dad and my other mom. But I wanted her to be home, so that I could talk to her.

Maddison S., 13
Daughter of a U.S. Coast Guard Mom:
My mom doesn't really go away for that long. It's only maybe a week at the longest. I just try to keep in touch, texting and calling. I also have my dad, and he's there too.

I know in other families, parents go away for months, but my mom doesn't really do that.

Khloe B., 13
Daughter of a U.S. Air Force Mom:
My mom was deployed when I was younger, and I don't remember that. But she has had to make trips. She is in the Air Force, a nurse practitioner, a teacher, and a student all at the same time. So, she is busy and travels for various reasons.

I'm not sure how I managed it when my mom was gone. I texted her and stuff like that. I would really try to distract myself while she was gone.

Maddie S., 15
Daughter of a U.S. Air Force Mom:
When she was deployed, it was hard. I remember that I cried a lot when she was first gone. We did get to talk to her, but it was always really early or really late. I remember her saying she had to wake up at 3:00 a.m. to call us, and she would go outside so she wouldn't wake anyone up. I remember one deployment when I was very young; I remember talking to her and asking her if she was saving our country.

Atiya J., 16
Daughter of a U.S. Navy Mom:
When my mom is gone, it is awful. The last time she left was hard; she was in and out a lot, but my mom is the one who keeps everything together. So, when she was gone, I lost my structure, and I got into trouble. It slowly got better.

Caleb C., 16
Son of a U.S. Air Force Mom:
When needed, my grandma comes down to help and offers extra support. My mom deployed to Afghanistan when I was younger. I don't really remember it.

The big one I remember was when she had to go TDY to North Carolina during COVID. That was bad because I was stuck here with my grandma and stepdad, who wasn't really a good guy. COVID was depressing enough, but with mom gone, it was horrible. During COVID, I didn't really have anyone to talk to.

D'Aaron C., 21
Son of a U.S. Air National Guard Mom:
Once, my mom deployed for a whole year. But she has a lot of training, which would require her to leave anywhere from a couple of days up to a week. Her TDYs are an ongoing, inside joke with us. It would be time for my birthday or something else, and she would head off for military duty.

This question is perfect because she just left last week, and she will be gone for two months. When she returns, she might be going on another deployment. She might be gone right up until my graduation, but she will make it back for my graduation.

Video games helped a lot. But you know, I could immerse myself in a good story and then play it. So, that was good, you know, YouTube, listening to music, finding new genres, playing football, usual stuff. Any activity to keep my mind off things.

Of course, I tried to call her as often as I could, to check in with her, because even when I know I am going through something, she is probably going through the same thing.

I try to keep my network open and use the time to become the best person I can, making good memories to share with her when she gets back.

Alexis Q., 29
Daughter of a U.S. Air Force Mom:
I don't really remember much about those times, as I was much younger.

Megan T, 28
Daughter of a U.S. Air Force Mom:
When I was one year old, both my dad and my mom were TDY to Korea, and they had just gotten stationed at Clovis (Cannon Air Force Base, New Mexico) after I was born, so they were still trying to find their people.

They left me with our neighbors on the base. And I ended up breaking my collarbone. And in Korea, like, this guy's like calling my mom and was like, "All right, Amy, don't have a cow, but your daughter is in the hospital." I don't remember too much about it, just from her telling me about it.

But when I was, like, sixteen, my mom was stationed in or was deployed to Afghanistan. She had just gotten engaged to my stepdad, and it was just my stepdad and me. It was like the first few months that we were alone together. He's figuring out things because he doesn't have any kids of his own. And he's trying to learn how to manage a sixteen-year-old without my mom's discipline.

She was only gone for six months, and I think that was the first experience I had of remembering her being gone. I was upset because I felt like she was moving on and leaving me with David. I thought, "she left me, and now I have to be around this man."

I remember always being so panicked because they would have these drills, which I don't know what they were called exactly, but they would have them when the Internet would cut off. One time, I was on Zoom with my mom, and then all of a sudden, my mom was gone, and we didn't hear from her for hours. It was, like, David and I looking at each other and like this poor man because I'm like, "Oh my God, is Mom dead?" He was like, "I don't know, but no." He just kept calm.

But it ended up being like such a great moment for David and me to really connect. You know, I think that all the time together was why I call him my dad now, because we spent so much time together back then. And, when she came back, I was like, "So, this is my dad, and you're chopped liver." [laughing]

And I remember her coming home being upset because the house was an absolute mess and her plants were dead. We definitely got in trouble when she came back.

Jamal Q, 30
Son of a U.S. Air Force Mom:
I don't quite remember my mom or dad leaving when I was young. But even when they both had to go, I was sure I had a fear of not knowing, but I didn't feel like I was being abandoned or anything.

You know that you have that community that your parents built; there were always adults checking up on us. I always felt comfortable with the people who would watch over us. Danielle (older sister) was also there for us. It was just like, "Okay, she'll be back." We talked to her pretty often when she was gone.

Also, I developed a sense of being able to do things on my own. I learned to take care of myself more quickly than if I were a regular kid. It's different when your parents are gone for two to three weeks or months.

Walker S., 30
Son of a U.S. Air Force Mom:
The first time, it sucked because it was right after my mom and my stepdad got married. My stepdad is like—he's one of my best friends now, and he is one of my confidants, and like, I can't imagine life without him in any way, shape, or form. But in the beginning, it was tumultuous. Like it always is with stepparents and stuff like that, right. So, uh, they were married for about a year when my mom got orders to go to the United Arab Emirates (UAE). Her first tour lasted four months, and later she had a second one for about six months, again back to the UAE.

The first one was super tough because my stepdad and I were already not seeing eye to eye on a lot of stuff. He's learning how to be a dad, and he was younger than I am now, like twenty-six or something, and I am learning how to have a dad for the first time in my life, so it was tough navigating that stuff. He would have to talk to my mom separately from me, and I'm sure I was acting up in school or doing something, not turning in reports or whatever it was. Man, how old was I? I must have been in fourth or fifth grade at that point, and they were, like, trying to co-parent while my mom was abroad. It was super tough.

I was still, somewhat, talking to my bio dad regularly. He was in the Marine Corps in Honolulu, Hawaii. I actually ended up flying over to Hawaii because I was eleven years old, and who wouldn't want to go to Hawaii? I went in the summer, and I spent quite a bit of time with him before coming back home.

I don't remember any specifics other than it being not easy, especially with my mom being a single mom for so long. It was really tough for me to lose her for that amount of time.

Even though the first one was tough for me, my stepdad and I had a much better relationship afterwards.

Myia E., 33
Daughter of a U.S. Air Force Mom
As a younger kid, it just sucks because, you know, it's just like she's gone. But, for a lot of her TDYs and stuff, I mean, I thought, you know, they were cool.

She went to Turkey and was gone for four months. I was in the fourth or fifth grade, and I didn't know how to deal with that. Like my mom was gone for months. Like, this person who I live with is gone, and now, I'm going to live with a teacher. So yeah, I did not handle that well.

I think that was the longest time she was gone until I was in college, and she went to Afghanistan. Then, it wasn't so bad because I was in college, but as a younger kid, the Turkey one sucked.

For the rest of the times when she was gone, I mean, they weren't terrible at all. And then I got older. I was able to stay at friends' houses and other places. Honestly, I was having fun, but then, of course, it changed my daily life. I had to adjust to whatever other people were doing instead of my usual routine.

And I have to give it to her because, despite all her deployments and TDY's and all that, she really made an effort to be at everything I did, and I was a busy child. When you get older, you do see that your parents made the effort. Like they tried to do as much as they could. Some kids had both parents in the home, and my mom was still somehow more involved than some other parents. Honestly, I don't know how she did it.

So outside of, you know, her leaving for a very long time when I was a child, the rest of it wasn't terrible at all.

Jennifer V., 38
Daughter of a U.S. Air Force Mom:
I don't know; It wasn't that bad. Looking back, it doesn't seem that bad because my mom didn't have to be gone for long periods. But it did seem like no matter when she had to be gone, something happened in that window. That is what made it feel like an inconvenient time, like even if she only had to be gone for three weeks, something would happen, and I would feel like, oh, I wish my mom was here.

But now, as an adult, a teacher, and a mom, I see that that's just how kids' lives are, with things constantly happening. So, when I thought this was just bad timing, any time would have been bad timing. A mom having to be away probably feels like bad timing to the mom and to the child. You get used to it. I mean, you do what you have to do.

The worst thing that sticks out the most is when she was gone, and I had picture day, and my dad had to do my hair. Oh my gosh, that was like the worst. Now it seems like such a small deal, but at the time, it was the worst. I cried after my dad did my hair, I cried when I got dropped off at school, and I cried after the pictures were taken. I was just like, "This is the worst hairstyle I could ever have for picture day."

It was nice that my mom didn't have to be gone for long periods. I do remember some people's parents, and even my dad, would sometimes be gone for a really long time. But my mom never had to be gone for months and months.

Chapter 7:
THE BEST PARTS

"My heroes are and were my parents. I can't see having anyone else as my heroes."[10]

— Michael Jordan

Military life isn't easy, but it's not all hardship either. For every challenge, there will be times of joy, growth, and pride. The military lifestyle comes with unique opportunities. The chance to travel, meet new people, and live in a variety of locations can result in some surprisingly wonderful memories. These experiences shape military brats into resilient, adaptable, and worldly individuals with exposure to diverse parts of the world and cultures. It introduces them to experiences many of their peers will never have.

I think one of the best things about military life is that our children learn early in life how to find the good in any situation. Maybe that's what helps them get through the tough times. It helps them focus on what they have instead of what they might be missing. This includes extended family, friends who have moved away, or one or both parents away from home because of military obligations.

Looking at my children and their experiences of life across the United States and around the world, I can recall many times they worked to find the good in every situation. I remember one of the times my husband and I were both had to go TDY and our kids got to stay with my sister and her daughter. They got to spend a couple of weeks hanging out with their cousin and enjoying life in Missouri. Turns out they focused on finding adventures where they were rather than the fact that mom and dad were gone. They're adults now, but those memories still bring smiles to their faces. Even moments that seemed difficult at the time often turn into treasured stories that still impact them today. As their parent, I am thankful that the good experiences outweighed the bad.

Being different isn't always easy, but sometimes it's the difference that becomes the gift. There was a time when being different meant you were on the outside or even ostracized, but thankfully, today, we are beginning to see that being different can bring a unique perspective or outlook. It helps you and others see and accept that we all bring something different to the table; our differences become a benefit to us and those around us.

Military brats often learn this early and develop a sense of independence and courage that serve them throughout life. They learn to make friends quickly, adapt to change, and appreciate diversity in ways others may not.

What each child considers "the best part" of military life will be different. It can change depending on age and location. For the young child, their circle is small and mainly involves those in their family and home. From that perspective, if things are good at home, then life is good. Even mom's absence can be a break in the routine and perceived as good.

For teens and young adults, the circle widens. Friends, school, and community experiences start to matter more. From this viewpoint, their community, neighbors, classmates, and friends can all influence what they consider good.

As young adults often gain a broader perspective, this can shift how they perceive their world. At this stage, they can become more self-aware, and their perception of what is good becomes more of an internal perception. They look back on their childhoods and see how those experiences shaped them, sometimes in ways they didn't realize at the time.

One external factor that impacts what seems good for a child is their parents' perspective on what is good. Children, especially younger ones, mirror the attitudes of the adults around them. If we, as parents, see each new move as an adventure, they're more likely to embrace it too.

The support or interactions with the community outside the military installation are also likely to change what a military brat feels. I think most communities' welcome military families because they realize the positive impact the installation and its members can have. A welcoming school, neighborhood, or local organization can make a positive difference in how a military brat adjusts to their new location.

This year I had the opportunity to work in our school district, and I saw administrators and teachers striving to make military brats feel seen and celebrated. Signs in the hallways said, Welcome Military Families, and teachers took extra care to acknowledge the sacrifices these kids make and the experiences they bring to the classroom. They participated in the Purple Up program, wearing purple shirts to show support. They even offered free yard signs to families showing support for their military neighbors. This kind of support can help children feel proud of who they are and where they come from.

In speaking with military brats, I found that the good parts of military life sometimes came from the very challenges they faced. On the one hand, a child might feel apprehensive about moving or their mother's separation, while on the other, they might look forward to the independence that comes with their mom being away. Moving meant leaving friends behind, but it also meant making new friends and seeing new places. Deployment meant time away from their military parents, but they also taught them to appreciate time together with family. Being different could mean being an outsider, but it can also help develop a unique outlook on life.

Of course, not every experience was easy, and as a military parent and now veteran, I can only truly see it from my perspective. But many military brats I spoke with said they wouldn't trade their childhood for anything. Here's what they told me about the best parts of growing up in the military.

Zoe B., 8
Daughter of a U.S. Coast Guard Mom:
Well, I got to meet a lot of people. If my mom wasn't in the Coast Guard in the first place, I wouldn't have as many friends as I do. And my mom wouldn't have as many friends either.

Blair S., 8
Son of a U.S. Coast Guard Mom:
It's probably getting free stuff. When I go to events with my mom, there is free food, and at the Exchange I can get things, discounts, and stuff like that.

Aniya Y., 8
Daughter of a U.S. Navy Mom:
I don't know.

Naomi M., 10
Daughter of a U.S. Air Force Mom:
I like traveling and being able to go on base.

Emma S., 13
Daughter of a U.S. Air Force Mom:
What I like most is being able to move and explore new places, meet new people, and try different foods. I like the newness of moving.

Maddison S., 13
Daughter of a U.S. Coast Guard Mom:
Definitely meeting new people that my mom works with and really just seeing what she does. When you go to all these events, it's just like I finally get to really see what my mom does.

I feel that now I'm more mature and I understand what she's doing and the impact she makes.

When I was younger, I would simply go with the flow. Now I see how important her job is and how much her job impacts the world, I guess.

Khloe B., 13
Daughter of a U.S. Air Force Mom:
I think the best part is somewhat bittersweet. I think the best part is getting to move to different places. Yes, it's really sad to leave your friends and the life you've built, but it is also kind of nice to experience other parts and cultures of the country.

Maddie S., 15
Daughter of a U.S. Air Force Mom:
What I liked most was just being a military brat. I didn't like it when people were faking sympathy. I could tell when someone was being genuinely nice and when they really didn't care.

Atiya J., 16
Daughter of a U.S. Navy Mom:
I like the vacations we take. We go on a lot of vacations.

Caleb C., 16
Son of a U.S. Air Force Mom:
Now that I'm older, the best part is definitely the benefits, such as the GI Bill and the military Identification card, which allows me to go on base if I want to.

D'Aaron C., 21
Son of a U.S. Air National Guard Mom:
For me, the best part was the whole experience, especially moving. I had to move so many times in my life. I have never lived in the same spot for more than four years, I think. Moving comes with having to make new friends everywhere, understanding different environments, and adjusting to something brand new every single time.

Alexis Q., 29
Daughter of a U.S. Air Force Mom:
I especially liked living in Japan, even though I didn't get to explore the country much as a young person.

Also, being able to make friends with a more diverse group of people.

Megan T, 28
Daughter of a U.S. Air Force Mom:
Is it like too easy to say that I think my favorite part was just the ability to go on base and have all of these things accessible to us and all of the resources? Because it was, like, a tough thing for me to adjust to once it was over and that was never going to be my life again? I couldn't go bowling for ten dollars or go to the Taj (a welcoming centerpiece for Randolph Air Force Base, often dubbed the Taj Mahal, housing the wing's administrative offices and the base theater) and watch movies.

I think really what I've loved most about being a military brat is just the experience that I've gotten to have through the military, the doors that it's opened, the number of people that you know have come into our lives. I think it's just been extraordinary, and I feel very privileged that I have this insight into the world that a lot of people don't get to experience. Yeah, I think that—yeah, that's the best part.

Jamal Q, 30
Son of a U.S. Air Force Mom:
As an adult looking back, the benefits were nice, especially the medical benefits. Traveling to different places was nice. Even now, I really like to travel.

I really enjoyed living in Japan. In the military, you always meet people who have lived overseas. So, we all have that in common. When I meet people who have no military background, it is a shock to them when I talk about living in Japan. A lot of them are amazed by that.

Also, just meeting a wide variety of people. That's huge. When you move a lot, you develop the ability to open up to the people you want to be friends with. It is also pretty easy to detach safely and move on. I think that is a skill I developed.

I am super grateful to have that experience because I don't think I would have done a lot of the things that I've done, the places that I've visited, or be as comfortable about traveling as I am now.

Walker S., 30
Son of a U.S. Air Force Mom:
While I was growing up, the best thing about it was that I always had friends. When I was in college, I always had friends to go back to. I traveled a lot for rugby; I still do. And to this day, I can call up a friend of a friend that lives in California, and we're playing a California team or in Colorado or someplace else. I can't go to a state where I don't know someone from my travels.

Luckily, I'm an extrovert, so I keep those relationships active over time too. I'd say what I liked about it, at the time, was the identity that I got on top of my folks' identities, if that makes sense. I was never a kid who would go around and use my parents' rank or something ridiculous like that. I think we all know military spouses or kids who would run around and be like, "My dad's a general" or whatever it was.

I feel more prepared for the real world than many of my peers. I didn't have a hard time adjusting; that's another part of what I do like now. Looking retrospectively, I felt much more ready for the real world.

Myia E., 33
Daughter of a U.S. Air Force Mom:
The different connections that it established because, honestly, now I have a lot more friends. I can start visiting more people I met in other states. My friends always tell me that I have family or friends everywhere. Or, asking me, "Where do you not know anyone?"

I have been exposed to different cultures. It's not as much of a culture shock to me, compared to someone who has never left their town, right? It's easier for me to adapt to people and situations; I think it has given me a different mindset.

I think that even being a military brat influenced my college choice. I chose the University of Houston because it's one of the most diverse schools in the United States. And I'm used to diversity, so I just kind of fit right in.

Jennifer V., 38
Daughter of a U.S. Air Force Mom:
What I liked the most was going to a lot of different places. And I don't know if everyone in the military goes to other places; I assume they do. But I liked that part.

It's really cool knowing that I have parents who have served our country. Everybody contributes to society in their own way, but I do think that some contributions are bigger, and some contributions feel bigger. And to know that my mom is making this contribution, that my mom's making this sacrifice. It just feels like my mom's life and her job are bigger than her. It's bigger than our family, and I think that's really special. And I even thought it was a special thing when I was a child.

But now, in hindsight, I think one of the best things is meeting different people from different backgrounds. So many people don't get to have that experience. If you live in a lot of other places and you meet a lot of various types of people at a young age, I think that it helps you to be more compassionate, more empathetic, and more accepting of others. Some people are stuck in the same area and only meet one type of person who all live the same kind of way, who all look the same, and all talk the same. It can get hard to see how all people share many similarities and it becomes easier to see the differences.

I appreciate that I grew up in a way that allows me to see and appreciate the differences in all sorts of people. And it wasn't something that I had to learn as an adult or something that I had to struggle with. It comes naturally to me because of the way I grew up.

Chapter 8:
THE WORSE PARTS

"I am prepared for the worst but hope for the best."[11]

— Benjamin Disraeli

In the military, as in civilian life, as often as we celebrate the good, we must also endure challenging parts. There is an old saying that goes, "Without the bad, you cannot truly enjoy the good." For military brats, that contrast between good and bad can be part of their everyday reality. Sometimes, the difference between what is good and what is bad is simply a matter of perception and time.

Military brats often miss out on the close ties that other kids have with extended family. They don't always get to spend weekends with grandparents or celebrate holidays with cousins. Sometimes, when they finally do visit family, they can feel more like strangers than family. As parents, we hope our attitude and the memories we create together help fill in those gaps. But longing for family is real, and not having ready access to their extended family can be challenging for military brats and may become more complicated as they get older.

While most military brats blossom where they are planted, some develop into introverts. While some take it as an opportunity to reinvent and reestablish themselves, others increasingly keep to themselves; they withdraw into their own world and avoid the pain and loss that is part of the military lifestyle. Each move, each TDY, each deployment, and each goodbye pushing them further into a shell. It can take years for them to break out of their shell and embrace their situation.

Another complex part of the military lifestyle is the feelings of sadness that can move into depression. Dealing with the ins and outs of being raised in the military can result in depression for some military brats. When dealing with depression and the continual cycle of military moves, getting help can be made harder by having to readjust and develop trust in those working to help them.

Throughout their childhood, military brats will inevitably face challenges that will seem unsurmountable. These challenges can be simple or complex but are still challenges. In the most demanding moments, military brats often develop strength and resilience, but that doesn't mean the journey is painless.

While every military brat might have a different answer for what they consider the worst part of their military lifestyle, I am sure they will also say, "But I made it through." The worst part today can bring growth and the strength to get through it. I believe it is even possible that, looking back, they might say, "It wasn't that bad," when considered in the context of their whole childhood.

The truth is that military life is filled with both the best and the worst. The challenges shape our children, just as much as the adventures. Here's what military brats shared with me about the worst parts of growing up in the military.

Zoe B., 8
Daughter of a U.S. Coast Guard Mom:
Being a military brat kind of got you a lot of attention, especially when you go to a new school or you move to a new community, and I didn't like having that attention on me.

Blair S., 8
Son of a U.S. Coast Guard Mom:
Straight up events. Because I don't know what is going on. I am just standing there, I have a lot of questions, and it's like, "What is this, what is that?" And it's like, "blah blah, blah." I don't know what anything means. But I do get to eat food.

Aniya Y., 8
Daughter of a U.S. Navy Mom:
I don't know. It's just hard.

Naomi M., 10
Daughter of a U.S. Air Force Mom:
There were times when my mom was not home but working. We would try to wait for her to come home to do things, but sometimes we just had to do it without her.

Emma S., 13

Daughter of a U.S. Air Force Mom:

I didn't always like moving. Sometimes, I wanted to stay in one place. I liked our last base, and I had to leave some friends behind.

Maddison S., 13

Daughter of a U.S. Coast Guard Mom:

My least favorite part is definitely moving. I feel like a lot of my friends stay in one spot for their whole life, and they'll say, "Oh, yeah, I've been here for fourteen years." But I don't really get a chance to say that.

I have a home, but I don't feel that I have a home that I have stayed in for longer than four or five years. So, yeah, moving is my least favorite.

Khloe B., 13

Daughter of a U.S. Air Force Mom:

I also think my least favorite part is definitely moving houses or having to leave my friends behind because leaving your friends behind is so hard. At this point, I am kind of numb to it, but at the same time, I don't like it. I can't explain it.

Maddie S., 15

Daughter of a U.S. Air Force Mom:

What I liked least was having my mom leave for any period of time. That was the worst part.

Atiya J., 16

Daughter of a U.S. Navy Mom:

I like the moves the least; I don't like having to move or leaving everything behind.

Caleb C., 16

Son of a U.S. Air Force Mom:

Pretty typical, I think, is the moving. You know, you make a great foundation, find all the people, and then you have to break the news to them that you're moving somewhere super far away. So, that would suck.

D'Aaron C., 21

Son of a U.S. Air National Guard Mom:

The worst part? Every time you settle in, it's time to move. The only thing I didn't learn was to decorate [laughs]. Every time I put up a poster or two, I'm like, "Oh well, time to move."

Alexis Q., 29

Daughter of a U.S. Air Force Mom:

I thought about it, and I don't have anything that I would consider the worst part.

Megan T, 28

Daughter of a U.S. Air Force Mom:

I loved all the access to the base and the things that we had on base, but that was also just in and of itself a challenge. Whenever I came out of that world, I was so sheltered, and I knew nothing different because I moved from Clovis (Cannon Air Force Base) at such a young age. So really, until I was eighteen, I was surrounded by the military and being on base, and that was hard.

I went to the University of Alabama on a whim, and I had no clue about the state of Alabama or what goes on there. And it was a very hard and shocking experience interacting with some of the people there. It was just not the military environment I was used to.

It was very sheltered, and it was just a tough transition that I don't think I got used to until my first job out of college.

Jamal Q, 30

Son of a U.S. Air Force Mom:

It's not necessarily something that I attribute to being a military brat, but it's a by-product. But seeing your friends leave often was something that definitely sucked. You know, social media today is not what it was then. Today, it is easier to stay in touch. I still talk to people that I have not worked with for a couple of years; it's super easy to keep in touch now. It was not always like that.

Also, having my parents go TDY, sometimes for long spurts of time. I am sure it was not great for them either. It had to happen, but still, not something I loved.

Walker S., 30

Son of a U.S. Air Force Mom:

What I like the least about it is that I was in a situation where I was being raised by a single mom. I didn't really have too many father figures or strong male figures until I was around eight years old. So, I felt that I really had to grow up pretty fast just because of that, let alone being a military brat. Being in that environment, you don't really get to be a kid a lot. You, like, lose a lot of being a kid and being able to mess up in those ways. Like when I hear stories about the trouble that some of my other friends got into in public schools. It was like, "What are y'all doing? You're going to get your parents in trouble." They're like, "What are you talking about?"

I felt like I had to hold myself to a different standard and responsibility because of, like, how serious it was to get in trouble. No underage drinking on base or even speeding or anything like that. It was like it was a different ball game growing up like that, and it was a different level of understanding and cohesion among us.

That's the part that sucked. In looking back, I especially think that I missed out on a regular childhood in a lot of ways. I had to grow up pretty quick.

Myia E., 33
Daughter of a U.S. Air Force Mom:
What do I like least about being a military brat? I think you know, part of that was just, like, separation and having to constantly start over. It was just a lot because back then, we didn't have all this technology. So you're trying to like, stay in contact with people that you knew from before, and all you had was a landline.

It made it practically impossible to stay in touch, unless you were writing letters. You start losing contact with a lot of those people. So, there were some missed connections or lost connections from that. The "having to start over" part sucks, too, because it's, like, once you build up all these relationships and stuff, and you have to move again and start all over again.

It has gotten easier with all the technology, and now there are so many people to try to keep up with. I get to pick and choose who I stay in touch with. But back then, it was just like, "I'll deal with who's in front of me, I guess."

Jennifer V., 38
Daughter of a U.S. Air Force Mom:
I don't want to say moving, but one move was hard, but I didn't like being so far away from family. Because it felt like so many things happened while we were gone. Every time we came back, I had to rebuild relationships. And that, I don't know, it just gets old, or it feels hard. I don't know.

I don't want to say uncomfortable because it was fine. But it did feel like everyone who lives in this place is together all the time. They see each other all the time. All of these things that happen, they already know about. We just missed a lot of things. Some things would have been nice to go to or to see with everyone else, but at the same time, I don't think I would have liked being there all the time either. I really enjoyed visiting Michigan City (Indiana), but I don't think I would have wanted to live there.

It was hard not seeing everybody all the time. I think it's probably easier now because there are things like FaceTime or Zoom. It just really wasn't like that for a long time, and if I wanted to, I couldn't even call because calling was expensive. I'd have to write a letter or send an email. I don't know. What thirteen-year-old really wants to email their cousins? Not me.

Chapter 9:
FOLLOWING THE MILITARY PATH?

"I don't want to follow in anyone's footsteps. I want to follow my own path and do something unique."[12]

— Kris Wu

While I am proud of the choices my own military brats made and their decision to follow their dreams, as their mom, I would have been happy to have them follow in my lead and choose a career in the Armed Forces. I am also sure that if they did serve, their talents would have been a credit to their service. My sister, also a veteran, felt differently; she didn't encourage her daughter to serve. Each parent sees it differently, and each child must choose their own way.

My children took different paths. Each of them chose careers that fit their own goals and dreams. Still, I believe military service is an excellent choice for many people; it certainly was for me. When I was fifteen, I already knew I would enlist in the Air Force. I made my decision based on what I heard from family members who had served, my desire to serve my nation, my favorite television show, and two years in the Junior Reserve Officers' Training Corps (JROTC). I even spent time at Space Camp in Huntsville, Alabama and stayed at a military installation while in JROTC. Those experiences help to cement my decision.

Children growing up in military families, on the other hand, have a unique opportunity to experience firsthand what it's like to be in the military without serving in uniform, to see this lifestyle from the inside before making that choice. Unlike my younger self, they don't just imagine military service; they see it up close. They see their parents go to work, they see them leave for extended periods, and they see them put themselves in harm's way. They see their actions, hear their words, and learn about the big and the small of life in the military. Every day, military brats see the choices and sacrifices that their parents make while serving. And like all children, they are bound to be influenced by their parents' career choices.

To some, the decision to follow in their parents' footsteps and serve in the Armed Forces is the natural thing to do. They may choose to enlist right out of high school or attend college and receive a commission into the Armed Forces because it is what they know, a sense of pride, or a means of furthering their education.

For others, life as a military brat may steer them away from serving in uniform. They are proud of their parents' decision and service but realize it is not the path for them. Their dreams may take them in a different direction.

Sometimes, they want to serve but can't. Medical issues or other factors may prevent them from joining. Even then, many find ways to give back to their communities in different roles, as teachers, civil servants, or in other avenues of public service.

There is no right or wrong choice; it's about choosing the best path for yourself. Here is what a few military brats had to say about following in their mother's footsteps and answering, or not answering, the call to military service.

Zoe B., 8
Daughter of a U.S. Coast Guard Mom:
Well. I think it would be fun to, like, be on boats and stuff. Something similar to what my mom did, it just sounds fun.

Blair S., 8
Son of a U.S. Coast Guard Mom:
I have already thought about it, and my plan is to be a pilot, either in the Air Force or Navy. I am going to fly the F-16 or F-18 (military aircraft), depending on which one I like. I am trying to think of which one I should fly. I have a simulator app on my iPad, and it's like a real simulator that has all the controls, so I can practice steering. It's really kind of fun.

I am also going to be an inventor. In case someone else starts to invent something similar, I will go straight to something else because I have a lot of ideas.

Aniya Y., 8
Daughter of a U.S. Navy Mom:
I don't think I will join the Navy because it looks hard.

Naomi M., 10

Daughter of a U.S. Air Force Mom:

I don't want to be in the military; I don't know why, but I don't want to join. There are things that I do want to do, but being in the military is not on the list.

Emma S., 13

Daughter of a U.S. Air Force Mom:

I don't know if I will join the military. I have a lot of things I want to do, but maybe I will join.

Maddison S., 13

Daughter of a U.S. Coast Guard Mom:

It's possible that I will join because I am pretty interested in the Coast Guard and the Armed Forces, but again, I don't want to move around. If I could find a job in the Armed Forces where I could stay in one place, then I would do it.

Khloe B., 13

Daughter of a U.S. Air Force Mom:

Would I join the military? One of the main reasons why I wouldn't join the military is that so many of my family members have been in the military. So, I kind of want a break from the military.

Another reason is I'm scared to be deployed and stuff. Whenever I see military movies or stuff, it's always about some war or something like that. It's like jumping out of planes, and my dad always tells me, like, that when he was like seventeen or eighteen, he joined the military, he had to jump out of planes and stuff, and that's why he's not a fan of roller coasters. Even my mom said she would prefer me not to join the military.

Also, I have my own dreams. I want to be an author, an actor, and an athlete. I want Khloe Best to be a name that is worldwide. When

I see myself, I see someone who is going to be famous.

I'm worried, though, that people won't take what I am saying here seriously, because what if other kids are more serious about what they are saying?

Maddie S., 15
Daughter of a U.S. Air Force Mom:
I don't think I will join the military. I don't want to have to leave all the time. And how would the military know what I want to be? Joining the military doesn't sound like something I would do.

I think I want to be a speech language pathologist, where I can work with children who are having a hard time learning to talk or have swallowing issues. I think it would be pretty cool to help kids improve their communication.

Atiya J., 16
Daughter of a U.S. Navy Mom:
I would not like to join the Armed Forces. Listening to my mom's boot camp stories and about being on the ship. it's not for me.

Caleb C., 16
Son of a U.S. Air Force Mom:
Following in my parents' footsteps: I have had this conversation with both of my parents. Most likely not really.

Actually, I'm going to a trade school. So, I don't think I would join. Maybe you know, it could be a last resort, but preferably not.

But, if I were, it would be for one reason, and that's the benefits. To allow my children to have a better future. And I would definitely want to go in as an officer, but I don't think I want to go to school for that.

D'Aaron C., 21

Son of a U.S. Air National Guard Mom:

I come from a family of military people: my great-grandfather, my great-uncle, my grandmother, my uncles, and my mom. It's a great legacy. But I don't think I will join the military. My mom doesn't want me to either. She joined to help provide for us, and given the current situation, it makes me want to pursue an education as much as possible.

I am not saying there is anything wrong with joining the military, and if I did join, I would join the Air Force. At the same time, I want to see what I can do outside the military.

Alexis Q., 29

Daughter of a U.S. Air Force Mom:

I did think about joining the military, but I am not the type that's cut out for such strenuous and early workout times. And you don't always get to pick the locations to which you will be PCS'ing.

Megan T., 28

Daughter of a U.S. Air Force Mom:

It's funny, my parents were like, "Do not join the military, please." They were like, "Go to college and get your degree." When I was in middle school, I was obsessed with the movie A Few Good Men. I always forget the actress's name, but I just wanted to be a lawyer in the military, whether it was in the Marines, Navy, or Air Force.

I also wanted to do an internship at a courthouse when we were assigned to Clovis or Cannon Air Force Base during my college years because I was still teetering with the idea of a career as a lawyer in the military. Then I actually interned at the courthouse and realized what they all do, and I was like, oh, never mind.

Also, as I got older, I thought, "Man, Mom, you work a lot and don't get a lot of say in what you do."

Jamal Q, 30
Son of a U.S. Air Force Mom:
Yeah, I think definitely as a kid, for sure, there's a small moment when I really didn't know what to do with my life or what I was going to do, and I thought, yeah, the military is always an option. And I think it's always. Whether this is a good thing or a bad thing, but , I don't know, but I think growing up as a military brat, you always know that's a backup option. That's something that I've seen up close enough to know that if I had to, I could do it.

Then, as I got older and I got away from the military lifestyle, I thought, okay, I still could join the military. That'd be really cool. Then I think about what it would take to be in the military. Then I am like, "Okay, I'm not doing that."

Walker S., 30
Son of a U.S. Air Force Mom:
My mom was the first female to join on her side of my family, but I came from a long line of service members. My parents instilled in me a sense of service and community. I tried to join at seventeen, but neither of my parents would sign the paperwork since I was under eighteen.

I was very much a rebel growing up, just like my mom. I needed the time to go to college personally. To grow up a little bit mentally and physically in a different way. I even joined ROTC in college.

After graduation. I was like, "I want all the cool parts of the military, but I've already reaped the benefits of a lot of the cool parts." The only thing I would need to join for was health insurance, but they let me stay on my parents' health insurance until I was twenty-six, which also influenced that decision.

Myia E., 33

Daughter of a U.S. Air Force Mom:

Join the Military? No, absolutely not! I wanted nothing to do with the military, to the point that I even refused to be in Junior ROTC in high school. And now, ironically, I'm a contractor with the Department of Defense. But that is the closest I will get to it; that's it.

Because I feel like I already served, I had to do all these things and deal with all this stuff, I didn't even ask for it. I was just born into it. And the constant moving is tiring.

Also, having a military parent, I think a lot of military parents have this mindset, like a soldier or officer mindset. Sometimes they tend to carry that home. So, I'm in that environment growing up, why would I want to go back to that environment when I can finally get out?

I feel like I have already basically served as a military brat. At this point, all you do is wait until you're twenty-six, then you lose all your insurance, the last of the benefits. It's like, all right, I already did my part.

When I was younger, we used to joke around about being a military brat. You are either going to hate the military or you're going to love it. There's no in-between. Those military brats who love it join right in because they know what they're getting into. Those who don't love it don't because they already know what it is going to be like.

I do think because I am a military brat, for my friends who have joined the military, that I have a better understanding of their lives than our friends who are not affiliated with the military.

Jennifer V., 38
Daughter of a U.S. Air Force Mom:
When you join the military, as I mentioned, you are doing something bigger than yourself, and it feels to me as if your life is not your own. And I didn't think that I could make such a big commitment and still be myself. But the older I've gotten, the more I know I probably would have been fine. But at the time, it seemed like there was no way I could do that.

I don't want to wear the same uniform every day. I didn't want to be stuck wearing my hair in a bun and putting on that hat every day. They tell me to move and I don't even get a say. I'd have to do whatever they tell me. And as someone finally reaching the stage of independence and being able to make my own choices, the idea of not having that autonomy was off-putting. But it's fine, and I liked it enough to even suggest joining the military to my husband.

It's not for me, but people should think about joining. I do think it is good for a lot of people. As a teacher, I don't suggest it for everybody, but I do recommend it for a lot of my students. If they say they are thinking about the military, I tell them, "If you're thinking about it, you should give it a try. It's not actually a lifelong commitment, just another thing."

It felt like it would be my whole life. I'm going to spend my entire life in the military because that's what my parents did, but you don't have to do that. You could get out when you want to get out. It seemed like a much bigger deal when I was eighteen and nineteen than it looks now, twenty years later. Now it seems like I could be out already. I could really almost be retired. If I had joined right out of high school.

I work with quite a few people who grew up in the military. None of them joined at all, but many of those who are fifteen or twenty years older than I am, have kids who are joining the military. I wonder if it's because we had an up-close look. A lot of us feel like we have already served our time.

Chapter 10:
ONE PIECE OF ADVICE

"You never really understand a person until you consider things from his point of view."[13]

— Harper Lee

Giving advice is easy. We do it all the time, we give advice to our family, friends, children, and our coworkers. We share lessons learned and try to help guide the people we care about. Sometimes they listen, sometimes they don't, but our intention is always to help.

As parents, advice comes naturally and we are always ready to offer it to our children, sharing the benefits of our experiences and wisdom. We try to help them learn from our mistakes rather than repeat them. Sometimes it works, but sometimes the best lessons are the ones they learn for themselves.

My oldest daughter is a teacher. She once had her high school students write a letter to their future selves. Her plan was to mail those letters to her students ten years later. The idea may have been to improve their writing skills but also to give them some perspective and a chance to reflect on who they were and who they had become. Perhaps when they receive their letters, those young adults will be reminded of their high school years, the goals they set, or the dreams they wanted to chase. The older self cannot respond, but maybe they will be reminded of forgotten dreams, first loves, or the completion of a journey that began long ago.

I thought what a gift these letters would be, to hear from their younger selves, to be reminded of their early life and their plans for their future. I also thought, wouldn't it be nice to be able to go back and offer your younger self some advice?

Unfortunately, we can't go back. But we can offer advice to people who are walking the path we once walked. When it comes to military life, who better offers advice to military brats than other military brats? They understand what it feels like to move, to say goodbye, to watch a parent leave for deployment. They know what it's like to grow up in a military family.

So, I asked them: If you could give one piece of advice to other military brats, what would it be? When I posed this question, I wondered what they would reflect on? Would they reflect on the good, the bad, or a little of both? Would they think of it as giving their younger selves a bit of advice or comfort? Well, here's the advice these military brats offered to those growing up as part of a military family.

Zoe B., 8
Daughter of a U.S. Coast Guard Mom
That, even though you might not see your parents much when they are away, that doesn't mean they want to be away; they have to do it.

Blair S., 8
Son of a U.S. Coast Guard Mom:
Just think of the good things, think of all the positives that could happen … like imagine the good stuff. Try to take advantage of it all.

Aniya Y., 8
Daughter of a U.S. Navy Mom:
I don't know what I would say.

Naomi M., 10
Daughter of a U.S. Air Force Mom:
I would say it gets hard sometimes, but it is also fun. If you are moving again, that might be a little hard, but you will meet new people.

If your mom is gone, it will get very hard and you will miss her, but know that she is coming back.

Emma S., 13
Daughter of a U.S. Air Force Mom:
Just enjoy it. When your mom is gone, consider calling or texting her when you can. Or even email her to just keep in touch.

Maddison S., 13

Daughter of a U.S. Coast Guard Mom:

I'd say you may think that in the moment, you might not like wherever you move or think you're not going to feel happy. But I always say, once you really get there, it's just like the same as always.

And my mom always said. When you move, wherever you go, you're going to make friends. And it is just like that because I'm a social person. I would just fit in anywhere.

If your parents have to go away, just be hopeful. I would say your mom is doing essential stuff for our world, and I would focus on the good things and the impact she's making. And when she comes back, all the stories she's going to have to tell.

Khloe B., 13

Daughter of a U.S. Air Force Mom:

I don't think I am the best person to give advice. But if I could tell myself about the move from Maryland, I would say, "It's not the end of the world, even though it feels like it is." I could say that to other military kids too.

Maddie S., 15

Daughter of a U.S. Air Force Mom:

I am not really good at giving advice, but one thing is to always talk to your mom. Try to look on the bright side and avoid focusing on the bad stuff.

If she is deployed, remember that she will come back. Remember to communicate however much you can, letters or texts, even if she is not able to reply right away.

When you are moving, try to make new friends. Don't forget about the past but create new memories wherever you are.

Atiya J., 16
Daughter of a U.S. Navy Mom:
When moving: It's going to be hard at first, but you will get used to it.
New to the military? Find something to focus on that you like and can do.

Caleb C., 16
Son of a U.S. Air Force Mom:
The main thing is that it sucks for the parents too. So be in it together.
It's just as bad for the mom as it is for the kid when it comes to moving,
babysitters, and going to a new school.

When it comes to your mom being gone? I don't know, maybe try
not to think about it too much.

You need to be really supportive because the military can be
pretty rough. My parents were both in the military and, unfortunately,
divorced. That can be hard; everyone has a different reaction.

D'Aaron C., 21
Son of a U.S. Air National Guard Mom:
My advice? I would say, learn to know and trust yourself, learn to set
boundaries, trust your gut, and learn to say no.

But also, learn to build relationships; these relationships can last
a lifetime and are important. Keep making friends.

You might be moving a lot, so really trust yourself and advocate
for yourself. Try to have a good sense of self. The words are not coming
out like I want them to. I am not sure this advice is suitable for younger
kids, but maybe as they get older.

Alexis Q., 29

Daughter of a U.S. Air Force Mom:

Enjoy the experiences while you can and make as many memories as possible (and don't forget to appreciate the available healthcare).

Megan T., 28

Daughter of a U.S. Air Force Mom:

Here is some advice I would have given myself when I was younger. Pay attention to the outside world—outside things like political things and just things in our environment—because that was the biggest shock for me when I went to college. I just felt like I didn't hear a lot of it when I was growing up. Things that go on in the world are different and overshadowed by what the military is doing.

I don't know if that's good advice. Honestly, take in the experiences that are a once-in-a-lifetime opportunity to be a military brat without the demands of military service.

My mom didn't go away very much, so I am not sure what advice I can give to someone whose mom has to be away. One thing I loved about my friend's family was that when her dad was home, her family made it a point to go out and do things and spend time together. I think when you are a kid, you don't value the time spent with your parents. Even my friend, Jamie, was annoyed when her mom made her do things with her dad.

I am very much about family time, and the best advice I can give is to make sure that when your parents come back, you hang out with them, because you don't know when is the next time they are about to leave. I think about the time my mom and I were on Zoom call and we got cut off, and I was like, "There she goes. She's gone forever."

My boyfriend, Louis, whose dad was in the military, says a good piece of advice is to find your group or community. When his dad was deployed, it was just him, his brother, and his mom, all by themselves. When his dad was gone, that is what his mom did: she found her own support network. Louis also found his own community for support. Even in high school, you can find your group, and this group can help you deal with whatever you're dealing with. They understand what you're going through and support you during your parents' absence. I think that's a good piece of advice … to find your own community or group.

Jamal Q, 29
Son of a U.S. Air Force Mom:
My advice: Take advantage of the opportunities to meet so many people. It is worth it. It's always going to be what you make it. If you're always against it and fighting it, it's always going to be hard.

If your mom or dad is away TDY or on deployment? I mean, it's hard to say anything because I can't say it's going to be okay, because you never know. What I would say is, as hard as it is for you, it's much harder for your mom when she has to leave.

Maybe you didn't sign up for it? But that's what your parents signed up for. So, if you make the best of it, it's not going to be that bad. I promise you. And you are going to meet so many people who are in the same boat as you.

Take full advantage of staying in contact with your friends when you do have to move and try all the different things. When you do move, especially if you're going out of the country. Take full advantage, like fully immersing yourself in the location and culture. That's one thing that my mom did. I'll say "forced" us to do when we were younger was getting fully immersed in the culture, and that is something that you'll be able to look back on and honestly appreciate because not everyone gets those experiences.

Being a military brat can be awesome. And it also looks pretty great on your resume when employers find out you're a military brat and you've been to all these places.

Walker S., 30
Son of a U.S. Air Force Mom:
I thought about this one for a while, about what I would want to hear from somebody. It's from my perspective as somebody whose entire family served, dating back to migrating over to the United States from Ireland and Germany. I wish somebody had told me that it was okay to forge my own path and to go a different route from the military. I was a firefighter, and that's how I served my community. I got a lot of reward from that, intrinsically and extrinsically. I did that during college, and that was huge. And it's okay to go the corporate path, or it's okay to go the contract route. It's okay to do anything that you want, and it's also okay if you want to go to the military. But my most significant piece of advice is to not let your parents tell you what to do when it comes to that stuff.

I guess my biggest piece of advice is to forge your own path, and it'll be super rewarding regardless of what it is. Go get a liberal arts degree, major in basket weaving, and if that's what your passion is, you'll find a way to make money off of it and find a way to survive.

I'm glad I did that, and I'm so happy that my parents weren't the ones telling me to join the military. They were actually telling me the opposite; they were like, "Hey, we joined, so you didn't have to."

I would say, go; go and do whatever makes you happy, and do whatever's going to make you successful and comfortable. That's treated me really well, and that's what I would say to another military brat.

Myia E., 33

Daughter of a U.S. Air Force Mom:

My advice: Make sure you have a hobby for yourself. I mean, it's cool to be in sports and stuff because I was a really active child and everything. But the thing about it is, when you have a lot of that team stuff, you have to constantly leave it. So, make sure you have a hobby that helps you get through all of these adjustments in life. I think that makes life a little bit easier, especially when it comes to transitions. Yeah, I mean, you can only do so much as a kid, but I think a hobby is the one thing that a kid can have more control over.

So, find something to ground yourself, to hold on to. Something that makes you happy. The thing that I've always had consistently is video games. Video games have helped me get through a lot of things in life. All these adjustments, especially when I'm dealing with a lot of these transitions. It helped me cope. But I mean, video games are not for everybody. However, I do believe that without video games, a lot of things would have been more difficult for me. I would also read a lot. Between video games and books, I was constantly in my own world.

Also, try to find something beautiful in each location that you visit or something to look forward to. Give yourself something to look forward to when it comes to each move, like learning about that area's culture. I mean, just getting outside.

When you get burnt out, it's okay to feel that. Like, it can feel like the same old, same old. You have to make new friends, and you get tired of it. When you feel like that, you really need to find the light at the end of the tunnel to help you and focus on that, whatever it is. It might help you get through it.

And talk to your parents. I feel like parents can help a child adjust to whatever is going on … a move, a deployment, whatever it is. Especially if they are going through something for the first time, their parents might be able to help them sort things out.

Jennifer V., 38
Daughter of a U.S. Air Force Mom:
If I could give them one piece of advice, it would really be to take advantage of every opportunity. One thing I really regret, especially as an adult, is that I didn't learn Japanese. Would I be using it now? No, but I could have?

I was there. I really had no reason not to learn the language, except that I genuinely did not want to. I didn't really want to be there. Even though I took Japanese in school, I didn't want to be there. My mom and dad thought it would be a good idea for me to take the class, and it never felt like it was my choice to do it, and I just was like, "Whatever. I'm taking this stupid class. I don't really care about this."

We lived there, I don't know, for six or seven years. I really could have learned a whole language, but I didn't. I could have gone to the snow festival, but I was like, "That's lame." I don't want to go, but how many United States citizens really get to go to the Sapporo Snow Festival?

My brother went to the snow festival, and we all could have gone. I was like, "Nope, don't want to go." I feel like I missed out on so many opportunities. Because I didn't see it as a big deal. But once you're outside of that situation, it's easier to see that even things that seem small or seem trivial are opportunities to grow. And I took some of those opportunities away from myself because I really didn't think they were important.

Something that we don't notice or don't realize, as children, is that some opportunities really only come once, and it feels like when you have so many opportunities that there's going to be just an endless number of opportunities in your entire life, that you can do that anytime, but that's not true.

When an opportunity presents itself, you should take advantage of it because you never know how it's going to change you for the better.

112

ACKNOWLEDGEMENTS

I want to acknowledge and thank God for His grace and blessings. I am thankful for the strength and the courage He has given to me throughout my life. It is my hope and prayer that He continues to guide me as I endeavor to inspire, motivate, and educate through thought-provoking works.

Thank you to all the military brats who contributed to this project. Thank you for your service and for taking the time to share your stories with me. I am honored to have you be a part of this journey.

Finally, a special thank you to my own military brats, Jennifer, Jamal II, and Alexis. Thank you so much for your "service," your love and support, and for allowing me to share your stories.

To all the literary professionals who have helped me make the book the best it could be. Your touches have added the polish that will allow this book to shine.

Neakail Tolbert used his skill and creativity to create the cover that captured my vision.

Marcus Griffin, who continually encourages me and pushes me to write daily and from the heart. Thank you for being my accountability partner.

Sara George added editorial expertise to this project. Her insights added authenticity and pushed me to new levels. I am thankful for her editing and her observations.

REFERENCES

Pat Conroy Facts for Kids of Kids Encyclopedia Facts. (n.d.). Retrieved on May 21, 2025 from https://kids.kiddle.co/Pat_Conroy.

Celebrating Military-Connected Children, Youth and Teens (n.d). Retrieved May 21, 2025, from https://www.defense.gov/Spotlights/Month-of-the-Military-Child/.

Quotes by Denis Waitley. (n.d.). BrainyQuote.com. Retrieved August 29, 2023, from BrainyQuote.com Web site: https://www.brainyquote.com/quotes/denis_waitley_165021.

'Military Brat:' Do You Know Where The Term Comes From? 10 Apr 2010. Katie Lange. Retrieved 27 January 2026 from, from https://www.war.gov/News/Feature-Stories/Story/Article/2060438/military-brat-do-you-know-where-the-term-comes-from/.

National Military Family Association (n.d.). Retrieved 2 February 2026, from https://www.militaryfamily.org/celebrating-military-kids-by-going-purple/.

Quotes by Ciara. (n.d.). BrainyQuote.com. Retrieved August 29, 2023 from BrainyQuote.com Web site: https://www.brainyquote.com/quotes/ciara_740559.

Quotes on military life – Action Speaks-Voices of Operation Homefront. (n.d.). Retrieved August 29, 2023, from Action Speaks-Voices of Operation Homefront. https://operationhomefront.wordpress.com/tag/quotes-on-military-life/.

Quotes by Paulo Coelho. (n.d.). Retrieved August 29, 2024 from, https://
www.goodreads.com/quotes/599176-if-you-re-brave-enough-to-say-
goodbye-life-will-reward#:~:text=Quote%20by%20Paulo%20Coelho%3A%20
%E2%80%9CIf,%2C%20life%20wil...%E2%80%9D.

Quote by Adam Stanley. (n.d.). Retrieved August 29, 2023 from https://www.
goodreads.com/quotes/7739354-no-matter-how-far-away-we-are-from-each-
other.

 Quotes by Michael Jordan. (n.d.). Retrieved August 29, 2023, from
BrainyQuote.com. Web site: https://www.brainyquote.com/quotes/michael_
jordan_158589.

Quote by Benjamin Disraeli. (n.d.). Retrieved August 29, 2023, from
BrainyQuote.com Web site: https://www.brainyquote.com/quotes/benjamin_
disraeli_154186.

Quotes by Kris Wu. (n.d.). Retrieved August 29, 2023 from BrainyQuote.com.
Web site: https://www.brainyquote.com/quotes/kris_wu_888070.

Quotes by Harper Lee. (n.d.). Retrieved 1 Aug 2025, from BrainyQuote.com
Web site: https://www.brainyquote.com/quotes/harper_lee_158272.

ABOUT THE AUTHOR

PATRICIA QAIYYIM was born in Michigan City, Indiana. She grew up in a large family living in locations throughout the mid-west and southern part of the United States. After high school, she attended college for two years before joining the United States Air Force. She served for more than twenty years on active duty. She has three siblings who also served in the Armed Forces.

As a member of the Air Force, Patricia had the opportunity to work in several specialties after basic training at Lackland Air Force Base in Texas and her initial technical training at Chanute Air Force Base in Illinois, Patricia's first assignment was Zaragoza Air Base, Spain, where she met her husband. Her other assignments included installations in Texas, Arizona, South Carolina, and Japan while raising their three children.

Patricia has always enjoyed a love of reading and writing. After many years of thinking about authoring a book about life as a mom in the military, she completed her first book, *Moms in the Military: Raising a Child while Serving in the Armed Forces* in 2022 and *Shrouded in Words: A Collection of Poetry* in 2023. She is currently working on her next literary project.

Besides reading and writing, Patricia is an avid quilter and enjoys everything crafty. She also enjoys cooking, working with her hands, and spending time with her family. She considers herself a woman of faith, a true Renaissance, and a citizen of the world. She believes we should all strive to inspire, motivate, and educate others as we move through life.

Patricia and her husband have three children, two grandchildren, and currently live in Texas.